IRISH CASE STUDIES IN ENTREPRENEURSHIP

Edited by Dr Cecilia Hegarty

Published by
OAK TREE PRESS
19 Rutland Street, Cork, Ireland
www.oaktreepress.com

© 2011 ACE Initiative

A catalogue record of this book is
available from the British Library.

ISBN 978 1 904887 49 2

Cover design by 2b : creative.
Printed in Ireland by ColourBooks.

CONTENTS

CASE STUDIES IN BUSINESS

CASE STUDIES IN SOCIAL ENTREPRENEURSHIP

FIGURES

TABLES

THE ACE INITIATIVE

The Accelerating Campus Entrepreneurship (ACE) Initiative is a joint collaboration of Cork Institute of Technology, Institute of Technology Blanchardstown, Institute of Technology Sligo and National University of Ireland Galway and is being led by Dundalk Institute of Technology. This project aims, through a collaborative approach, to create entrepreneurial graduates. The ACE Initiative recognises that, to encourage and sustain a vibrant, successful knowledge economy, Ireland must increase the number and quality of indigenous companies and create graduates, irrespective of discipline, who are entrepreneurial thinkers and doers. The ACE Initiative therefore seeks to explore how the Higher Education Institutions in Ireland can develop and deliver a framework for embedding entrepreneurship education across all disciplines to fulfil the aim of "Creating the Entrepreneurial Graduate". This will require not only embedding entrepreneurship education into existing non-business programmes but also effecting organisational change within and between the institutions to reflect entrepreneurial processes. This involves collaboration between the academic Schools and Departments, Incubation Centres and Technology Transfer Offices.

The ACE Initiative is part-funded under the Strategic Innovation Fund by the Higher Education Authority in Ireland, which is funded by the Irish Government under the National Development Plan 2007-2013 with the assistance of the European Regional Development Fund. It also is co-funded by its partner institutions and, from its conception, has had support from Senior Management across all partner institutions. The ACE Initiative has evolved from a growing perception that the traditional approaches to teaching entrepreneurship are not suited to the challenge of creating the entrepreneurial graduate. This book, which deals with both commercially- and socially-oriented cases, is one of a number of valuable outputs of the ACE Consortia. The ACE Initiative has resulted in collaboration between departments and between institutions to co-develop and co-deliver entrepreneurship modules and fully-fledged programmes in non-business disciplines from levels 6 to 9. It would be remiss not to mention additional outputs of the ACE Consortia, including the Student Internship Programme, Train the Trainer Programmes for Enterprise Educators, and Leadership Development Programmes.

THE CASEBOOK

This ACE casebook provides a range of live case studies that are suitable for use in entrepreneurship education and training. The case studies should be particularly useful in Higher Education Institutions in Ireland and in the international context. These case studies can be employed to enhance the student's practical understanding of the theory of the entrepreneurship process and new venture development. The cases are related to the enterprise issues faced by organisations and individuals from diverse industry sectors. The publication includes teaching material from the social enterprise sector to high technology start-ups, to graduate businesses. The cases are written by staff at the teaching interface, by recent graduates, and by experts and mentors involved with growing commercially-viable ventures. A significant achievement of this casebook has been to encourage contributions from practitioners who tend not to publish but have a wealth of experience in working in or with small to medium-sized enterprises (SMEs) or charitable organisations.

On behalf of the ACE Consortia, I would like to encourage all enterprise educators to use case studies as part of their pedagogical toolkit for delivering enterprise education. The editor has endeavoured to bring together a number of cases that highlight the dynamic process of entrepreneurship, whether this is in a new start-up, a community venture or a long-established business.

The first case in this book outlines the practice of ethical entrepreneurship, while at the same time building a lucrative market for Java Republic products. Operating in the food and retail sector, David McKernan is faced with some tough branding, production and market expansion decisions.

In the second case, the Lenihan brothers have used their experience in the telecoms industry to set up Phones Made Easy in Kilmallock, County Cork. The case documents how entrepreneurs must be ready to adapt to a changing marketplace and it provides an insight into some of the challenges associated with franchising.

Mcor Technologies is the focus of the third case. Here, the case writer portrays the story of a family business based in Ardee, County Louth, which strives to compete on the world technology stage with the likes of Sony,

Motorola and Amazon. The MacCormacks risk secure jobs and more to fund their invention, the Matrix, a new 3-dimensional printer. Mcor Technologies is a perfect example of a disrupter; the MacCormacks demolished the *status quo* of rapid prototyping through additive technologies.

The Galway Hooker represents the only case in this casebook written by a postgraduate student. The Galway Hooker, founded in 2006 by two cousins, Aidan Murphy and Ronan Brennan, is a brand of Irish pale ale brewed in County Roscommon. It is currently only available in Ireland on draught in pubs mainly in and around Galway, with selected outlets in Cork and Dublin. This case provides good insight into growth within a niche market.

Amray Medical describes the journey of Helen Johnston, from radiographer to international entrepreneur. Amray Medical manufactures a patented range of X-ray protection aprons for use by radiographers and is now a reputable niche player in the medical supplies industry. The Johnstons, Helen and her son, William, are a true example of entrepreneurial can-do attitude; Helen spotted an entrepreneurial opportunity over 20 years ago and, since William joined her, the company has been building on its key strengths ever since.

Íompar Logistics tells the story of the 'incubatee', Gerry Bedford. Gerry established Íompar Logistics as a global provider of freight payment services and transport management solutions in 2005. This company increases the bottom-line performance of its customers through operational efficiencies. The case will be useful to those seeking to understand better the start-up processes leading to growth.

The final case in the business section of this book is the story of SL Controls, a Sligo-based engineering company It was founded in 2002 by Shane Loughlin and Keith Moran, both of whom met at IT Sligo in 1998 in their roles of engineering lecturer and student. This case illustrates the challenges of bringing a new innovative process, DiVOM, to the marketplace.

In the second section of this book, social enterprise cases are presented. The first case describes the entrepreneurial journey within the community enterprise context. The industry sector is tourism. This is a deliberately 'messy' case, highlighting the many key actors involved in community-based ventures and the need to make decisions based on multiple stakeholders. The case illustrates the difficulties of managing a venture with limited resources but emphasises the positives of working together and sharing resources in true community spirit.

In the final case, the case writer provides an account of the inspirational Lifestart Foundation, which seeks to offer children a better start in life through education. Lifestart was established in 1980s by a school teacher, Sister Delores McGuiness, who commanded the support of numerous volunteers to grow the Foundation into a nationwide body. Although Lifestart is now a national charitable organisation, it continues to rely on its core volunteers, which presents all sorts of challenges in a voluntary sector with diminishing government sector funding. The story is a compelling account of the diverse issues affecting growing social enterprise ventures.

A number of cases in this ACE casebook have already been trialled with students in third-level education in Ireland. Four of these cases were used during the local and national finals of the 2010/2011 Newstalk 106-108fm Student Enterprise Competition. Launched in 2006, the Newstalk 106-108fm Student Enterprise Competition is designed to develop an understanding of business management and to promote early-stage entrepreneurship among third level students. Using a case study format, the competition allows participants to research Irish companies and, as part of a team, to devise solutions to real-life business scenarios. The competition chairperson, Mr Denis O'Brien, recently acknowledged "... the importance of case studies when learning and teaching entrepreneurship. Textbooks often can be difficult to digest. Case studies give a great insight into the minds of entrepreneurs and the decisions they make on a day-to-day basis".

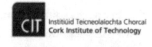

THE EDITORIAL BOARD

THE CASE WRITERS

DEIRDRE BANE has a PhD in Entrepreneurship, is a member of the Association of Chartered Certified Accountants (ACCA) and holds a Masters of Arts in Public Administration. She currently holds positions at the Institute of Technology Blanchardstown and National College of Ireland.

AISLING CONWAY is a lecturer in Economics in the Department of Continuing Education at Cork Institute of Technology. She is also a member of the Academic staff in the Centre of Policy Studies at University College Cork. Her research interests include regulation and small business.

GARRETT DUFFY has held senior management and engineering roles in multinational corporations in Ireland, the UK and France. An electronics graduate (DkIT) and a business studies graduate (IPA), he has been a serial entrepreneur. Garrett joined DkIT in 2006 as a lecturer and now works in the Regional Development Centre as Enterprise Development Manager, supporting over 100 start-up technology entrepreneurs.

ROSE LEAHY is a lecturer in Marketing in Cork Institute of Technology. She is co-editor of the *Irish Business Journal* and has published both academic articles and case studies nationally and internationally. Her main research interests are in the areas of marketing and advertising.

SEAN MAC ENTEE, B.E., M.Sc., M.B.A., is Incubation Centre Manager at the Regional Development Centre (RDC), which is DkIT's innovation support and technology transfer organisation. Prior to joining the RDC, Sean spent over 20 years managing his own engineering company.

CAROL MORAN is a lecturer of Economics and Marketing at the Institute of Technology, Sligo. Carol has previously worked in the marketing industry, providing services to national and global companies and is the current Chair of the North West division of the Marketing Institute of Ireland.

SEÁN O'COISDEALBHA qualified as an industrial chemist from UL and also holds a Grad.Dip. in Quality Management (NUIG) and a MBA (IT Sligo). He started his working career as a quality assurance system validator in various companies, before working as a Development Executive Officer with Údarás na Gaeltachta. He is a founding director of Ionad Ealaíona Iorras Teo.

DOIREANN O'CONNOR holds a BA in Applied Social Care, MAs in both Education and Public Management and is in the final year of a Doctorate of Education at the University of Sheffield. She is a lecturer in Early Childhood Care and Education at Institute of Technology, Sligo, teaching undergraduate BA students and supervising Research MAs in social and educational-related fields. Doireann had her own R&D business, prior to entering academia.

CATHY O'KELLY is a lecturer in Business at the Institute of Technology, Sligo. Cathy has worked with a number of multinational organisations. Her current research interests include advancing problem-based learning approaches to education, entrepreneurship and the development of innovation within the SME sector.

NOLLAIG O'SULLIVAN is a lecturer in Management at Cork Institute of Technology. She has published case studies nationally and internationally and her main research interest is in the area of strategic management.

PAULINE RIDGE has national and international marketing experience, gained while working for companies such as Heineken and Nestlé. Pauline has managed product brands and led teams in new product development. She is currently studying for a post-graduate diploma in enterprise management at NUIG.

PAT SCANLON is Head of the Department of Business and a lecturer in Marketing Management at Institute of Technology, Sligo. Pat holds an undergraduate degree (Trinity College Dublin) and three Masters degrees: Master of Arts (Trinity College Dublin), Master of Social Science (Queen's University Belfast) and Master of Arts in Enterprise and Technology (DkIT). He is a Fellow of the Marketing Institute of Ireland. His research interests are in strategic marketing management, non-national entrepreneurship, third-level education management, foreign direct investment and government policy.

JOHN SISK is a senior lecturer in marketing at DkIT, and has developed and delivered on a wide spectrum of marketing programmes for both undergraduate and postgraduates. John is a Commerce graduate (University College Cork), and has a Masters in Marketing (University College Dublin). He is also a member of the Marketing Institute of Ireland. He has held positions in the Irish Dairy Board, Enterprise Ireland and University College Dublin. He is a visiting lecturer to partner colleges in Europe.

MICHAEL WALSH is a senior lecturer in the Department of Management and Marketing at Cork Institute of Technology. His research interests are industry clusters, new business formation and growth, and marketing communications.

CASE STUDY TEACHING NOTES

Case teaching notes are available for all the case studies in this book from the editor, Dr Cecilia Hegarty (email: cecilia.hegarty@dkit.ie, tel: 042 937 0422 / +353 42 937 0422).

PREFACE

Entrepreneurship is finally something that we're proud of in Ireland. We've realised that it's at the core of our economy, which is a great thing.

It may seem very obvious, but we're an island, with a substantial and dispersed infrastructure and a very small population. So we're never going to be a cheap location.

If there are three words that are musts for any new global entrepreneurial enterprise today, they have got to be: faster, better, cheaper.

... which means we must be disrupters. As entrepreneurs, we need to create business models that demolish the *status quo*. We need to craft visions that avoid us becoming disruptees (an entrepreneur who is demolished by a disrupter).

Sustainability is important, so whatever we are developing, we must envision what we are doing several iterations ahead. In doing so, we need to have a set of core values and reasons for what we are doing.

Do we passionately believe that we can make life better for customers with what we are creating? When we spin the clock forward five years, is it likely that we will have evolved enough still to add substantial value?

We must be honest with ourselves about the space we are entering – not on a local or national level, but on a global plane. Because it is globalisation that is our greatest threat *and* our greatest opportunity.

None of this is the responsibility of Government or society. In the most charming way, true entrepreneurs hijack all sorts of resources to create an advantage for their vision to succeed. We take responsibility for what we are undertaking ourselves.

As Irish entrepreneurs in troubled times, we should not be found wanting. A new sort of patriotism is required to leverage our education, heritage and intellect to create an Ireland that will ride the crest of the wave of globalisation rather than allowing it to crash painfully down on top of us.

Jerry Kennelly
Founder
Tweak.com

CASE STUDIES IN BUSINESS

1

INTRODUCTION

Entrepreneurship is one of the cornerstones of a modern economy and the lifeblood of thriving local communities. As the economic environment hardens, growing our own enterprises has never been more important. We know that, particularly in tough times, it is small new firms that create jobs. The case studies featured in this section of the book give an excellent insight into the types of entrepreneurs and businesses that Ireland needs to rebuild its economy. This initiative by ACE is an important building block in developing the skills of the entrepreneurs of the future who we need to accelerate the strong momentum of the last decade when entrepreneurs established businesses in every town and county, showing exceptional ambition and innovation to start up, grow and internationalise their businesses, thus creating wealth and jobs at home in Ireland.

Entrepreneurs are absolutely central to the rebuilding of Ireland's economy and they are a huge national asset, which needs to be nourished. Ireland is a highly entrepreneurial society and entrepreneurship is exceptionally strong here. We are ranked significantly higher than the European average and established entrepreneurs make up 9% of Ireland's population. We have a higher proportion of established entrepreneurs than Germany (4%) the UK (6.1%) and the US (8.3%) and about the same level as Finland (9.2%).

This strong entrepreneurship culture makes Ireland an attractive place to do business. This is endorsed by the World Competitiveness Rankings, which place us in the top 5 for corporate taxes, being open to new ideas and for the availability of skilled labour. We are in the top 10 for labour productivity, for the availability of financial skills and, most importantly, for the flexibility and adaptability of people. The support infrastructure for entrepreneurs is very broad, with advice and funding delivered locally by the County and City Enterprise Boards. Indeed, the programmes for high potential start-ups offered by Enterprise Ireland are regarded by the EU as 'best in class' and a model for other European countries.

The environment for new business start-ups is strong. Modern incubation space is available throughout the country and third-level colleges across Ireland are playing a very important role in helping technology-based businesses to incubate and grow by providing flexible working environments, supported by services and skills development.

As it becomes more and more difficult for European and US companies to compete with Asia on price, innovation becomes the key to success. Ireland is meeting this challenge and has developed a very dynamic research, development and innovation sector, driven by an exceptional level of collaboration between industry, academia, government agencies and regulatory authorities. A recent survey showed that almost 50% of all enterprises in Ireland are engaged in innovative activity, placing us 7th across the EU and considerably above the EU average of 39%. However, all companies must innovate if they are to grow and prosper. Entrepreneurship is not just about start-ups – it's about entrepreneurship and innovation throughout the life of every company.

It is essential that we trade our way out of this difficult time. As our home market is too limited to grow the economy, we must trade internationally. Ireland is a small country and, from day one, Irish companies must think internationally. This gives us a head-start, as we are experienced in exporting much earlier than our competitors in the UK or Germany, where they have such a large domestic market.

In the Irish economy, exports equal jobs. We are an exporting nation, we sell over 80% of all that we produce overseas. The answer to Ireland's challenge remains a return to the export-led growth that drove the economy in the foundation stages of the boom.

Our export engine of high quality, competitive companies is fundamental to Ireland's return to growth. These companies play a significant role in stimulating local economies and employment, fostering the climate of innovation and translating Irish entrepreneurial ambition and potential into commercial reality. It is critical that they are supported to position themselves to increase their international market share and to capitalise on global opportunities. To grow, these indigenous businesses need assistance to develop their management and innovation skills as well as improving their competitiveness through the most modern techniques, such as lean manufacturing.

Many of the world's best companies such as Google, HP and Microsoft were born during difficult economic times. Irish companies that did not exist 10 to 15 years ago now employ hundreds of people and are recognised as leaders in their fields, they are selling products and services into world-leading companies right across the globe.

In Ireland today, there are significant opportunities for new business start-ups, particularly in life sciences, bio-tech and medical technology, cleantech engineering, food, telecommunications, internet services and other niche areas. These are businesses with a solid focus on knowledge, innovation and research and development and the capability to establish strong positions in international markets, sustain international competitiveness and achieve export growth.

Developing the entrepreneurial culture regionally and supporting innovative, export-focused start-up companies is a key national priority. Enterprise Ireland is the Irish government's lead agency responsible for the development and growth of the indigenous business sector. There is a full range of supports available for entrepreneurs with new and innovative business ideas to explore all aspects of setting up an export-oriented business and to determine whether entrepreneurship is the right course for them.

I welcome this casebook produced by the ACE Initiative. The world of entrepreneurship relies upon today's graduates having a sound understanding of the principles of entrepreneurship so they can embrace this career pathway should they choose to. Entrepreneurship education should be a must for all third-level graduates, regardless of their discipline of study; this casebook provides educationalists with a useful pedagogical tool to engage students in the real-life practicalities of enterprise development.

Pat Maher
Executive Director
Enterprise Ireland

2

JAVA REPUBLIC COFFEE ROASTING COMPANY

Rose Leahy and Nollaig O'Sullivan

CASE SYNOPSIS

Irish consumers in recent years have developed a taste for coffee and its many variants such as cappuccinos and lattes. This demand has fuelled significant growth in the premium and speciality coffee sectors. Capitalising on this opportunity, Java Republic Roasting Company was the first specialty coffee roastery to enter the Irish market for over 100 years. This company was set up by David McKernan in 1999, with a staff of eight at a 5,500sq ft roastery in the City Link Business Park in Dublin.

Having enjoyed many successes to date, Java Republic now finds itself faced with a global recession, increased competition and significant below-capacity production at its new roastery. Decisions have to be made regarding the future strategic direction of the company. Options such as investment in retail, franchising and expanding into Europe and beyond are some of those open to Java Republic. In making these decisions, David is adamant that Java Republic will not compromise on the fundamentals of openness, integrity and social responsibility to origin countries and demands careful future strategy development founded on the company's ethos and values.

INTRODUCTION

Of all of the things that could have prevented David from attending his monthly management meeting, he never thought that volcanic ash would be one of them. However, sitting in the airport in Toronto, waiting for a return flight to Ireland, gives him extra time to consider the best way for his company to proceed.

Since David began Java Republic in 1999, it has become one of the fastest-growing coffee brands in Ireland. While there have been many obstacles along the road, the business is now well-established. With a current turnover in excess of €6.9 million a year, the company is still plotting expansion. The growth to date is impressive, particularly considering that he started out at the kitchen table, and nearly lost his house in the process. He admits to making every mistake in the book, but he kept going.

While proud of the past, David has concerns about the future direction that Java Republic should take. With the changing economy and more competitive industry landscape, David McKernan and his management team have some hard decisions to make. Ensuring that the company maintains and grows its market position, without sacrificing quality and its current reputation, is not an easy task.

ENTREPRENEURIAL BACKGROUND

David is a business entrepreneur. Leaving school, he went straight into a successful career in one of Ireland's main coffee retailers, Bewley's, and there learned the trade as sales and marketing manager. After 12 years, he knew it was time to venture alone, and so went on to set up Java Republic Roasting Coffee Company in 1999. David McKernan was the first independent to take on the main players in Ireland's coffee market in over 100 years.

David McKernan established his own set of ethical principles about the sourcing of his coffee, much of it inspired by the shock he felt when he first visited impoverished farmers. David is known for his strong opinions, most notably in his demands for fair treatment of coffee and cocoa growers and he has no time for unfair practices that typify the coffee industry: "I want to know that our business is based on sound principles and I don't want anyone ever to be able to say that Java Republic is screwing the producers, the small farmers who collectively put our coffee into the market-place".

In 10 years, David has started, grown, developed and guided his vision to a successful and prosperous business, all the while maintaining an openness in communication and ethics that is virtually unheard of in the coffee industry. Now David has turned his attention to questions of environmental sustainability. He set out to create the 'first carbon-neutral coffee roastery on the planet' just outside Dublin and has won an environmental award for it. There is an open invitation to any interested operator or customer to visit the roastery.

Despite his ethical and environmental concerns, David believes that life is to be enjoyed. He takes regular holidays abroad with his family, has a beautiful house and fancy car – all the trappings that his business success has enabled. However, he continues to maintain a fierce commitment to the values of Java Republic.

By his own admission, David is someone who has always done things a little differently: "I thought I'd have enough money to set the business up, that I'd be able to get the investors in and build the business and everything else. And it ended up taking me one full year before I produced one case of coffee. And I started off in September 1999 with eight other people and no customers, which in hindsight was probably the wrong way to do it – but it eventually worked".

Some of the attributes that have taken David to where he is today have been his focus and persistence. David is extremely confident, and has always been prepared to attack competitors who he believed were selling both the customer and producer short. It seems that despite the knocks, it is his confidence in his ability to succeed that keeps him buoyant.

BUILDING THE BRAND

In 1999, with a staff of eight at a 5,500 sq ft roastery in the City Link Business Park in Dublin, Java Republic was born. In 2007, the company raised €1 million through a Business Expansion Scheme and was backed with €6 million from Bank of Ireland to build a new premises in Ballycoolin, Blanchardstown, Co. Dublin. By September 2008, Java had moved location to this new manufacturing facility. This is a purpose-built 23,000 sq ft coffee roastery and comprises a manufacturing plant and a restaurant /café (see **Appendix 1**). It has been built to European regulation standards in terms of building fabric insulation, ventilation and heat loss and has the aim of being the world's first carbon-neutral coffee roastery. People who visit the roastery can drink Java's beverages while watching the roasting process through a glass wall and learning about its ethical approach to business. This 'coffee house' not only allows Java to share its philosophies with the wider coffee-drinking population, it also happily coincides with a 10-fold increase in Java's production capacity enabled by the new facility.

David believes that the roastery has reinvented the café experience by giving customers a front row seat to the theatre of handroasted coffee. What might simply have been a facility to increase capacity instead becomes a tangible, memorable and emotional experience. This facility to produce carbon-neutral coffee is central to the ongoing development of the brand image, which is founded upon the roasting process that David patented in 1999. When questioned about the Java brand image David outlines the key factors that differentiate Java's coffee from the competitors. These he describes as their unique selling points (see **Figure 2.1**).

As is evident from **Figure 2.1**, one of Java Republic's unique selling points is 'Coffee with a Conscience'. Java markets itself as a buyer of ethically-sourced coffee, tea, cocoa and sugar, referring to the people who grow their ingredients as 'our partners in excellence'. This has always been one of David's driving principles, and while others may have their doubts about coffee production and ethics, the 'Coffee with a Conscience' tagline is central to the belief held by the company that ethical sourcing and quality can and do go hand-in-hand. Under the Coffee with a Conscience programme, Java Republic is committed to sourcing the best quality beans at a fair price. This commitment to ethical trade includes fair-trade coffee and direct partnerships with farmers and co-operatives.

Figure 2.1: Java Republic's 10 Unique Selling Points

1.	**Better Green Beans**	Java Republic only uses Grade 1 Arabica Green Beans in its blends (most companies use the cheaper Robusta beans along with Arabica to bulk out the coffee).
2.	**Handroasted**	Java Republic does not use computers to roast its coffee. Each varietal is handroasted by craftsmen.
3.	**21 Minute Slow Roast®**	Java Republic roasts at a low heat, for a long time – 21 minutes. This produces a dark, rich roast with a strong sweet flavour.
4.	**Origin Flavour Lock®**	Each of Java Republic's 26 Grade 1 bean varietals has a unique flavour characteristic, so Java Republic handroasts every one separately before blending.
5.	**Naturally Cooled**	Java Republic ends its roast by stirring handroasted beans in an open tray; they cool slowly, which protects and enhances flavour.
6.	**Date Roasted**	The coffee is fresh produce – so it is packed straight after roasting and the date and time of the roasting is displayed on packs. This is vital, because once roasted, coffee has a relatively short life.
7.	**Unique Grind**	Most coffee companies sell only one grind for both plungers and filter coffee machines. David McKernan believes this 'multi-grind' is a short-cut that destroys flavour. In order to avoid this, Java Republic grinds its coffee beans to a specific size for plungers or filter coffee machines.
8.	**Fresh Valve Technology**	Because fresh roast coffee releases gases, Java Republic's pack has a one-way valve. It lets the coffee breathe, yet protects flavour. Other roasters have to wait days before packing.
9.	**Coffee with a Conscience®**	Java Republic gives 11% of net profits to projects in coffee-growing communities, and it only buys from recognised ethical traders or from sustainable co-ops.
10.	**Carbon Neutral Coffee**	Java Republic operates a carbon-neutral roastery, in Ballycoolin, Blanchardstown, Co. Dublin.

In a move that could lead to more change and balance for the farmer, Java Republic has decided to be the first coffee company to openly declare the

International 'C' Commodity price of coffee per pound. This then can be compared to the minimum price, average price and the price of fair-trade coffee paid by Java Republic per pound of green bean. In forging direct partnerships with coffee producers, farmers at the Kuapa Kokoo co-operative in Ethiopia, for example, are paid a fixed rate above the fluctuating market price for the cocoa they produce, including a bonus based on the co-op's profits. They also benefit from health insurance and educational support for member families, in addition to a social premium of €150 per tonne paid by Java Republic to support community programmes. Other initiatives undertaken by Java Republic to better the plight of coffee-growers include the 'Fancy a Drink Anyone' Illili Darartu (a village in the Ethiopian coffee region of Harar) Charity Evening. The evening and subsequent donations raised €170,000 towards a water plant for the supply of fresh water for the people of the Oromia Co-operative in Ethiopia. To put this money to effective use, Java Republic has linked with Plan Ireland to develop the water project in the region. Java Republic's objective is to support co-operatives such as this by increasing trade through the purchase of green beans and by contributing to community projects. David has also set up the Java Republic Foundation, which pays 11% of the company's net profit to coffee-growing communities. Following the earthquake in Haiti, Java Republic made a decision to help the country through a 'trade-out' instead of a 'hand-out' by purchasing approximately $100,000 of Haitian coffee. While making moves to balance the inequalities currently experienced in the coffee industry can be regarded as admirable, others have questioned whether a need for such ethically-sourced coffee exist, and whether the company's commitment to ethics might come at the expense of profits?

COMPETING WITH THE BRAND

The fresh coffee market is Ireland is dominated by four main players: Bewley's (est. 44%), Kenco (est. 15%), Robert Roberts (est.12%) and Java Republic (est. 12%), with the rest of the market made up of independent coffee roasters and distributors. While Java Republic has carefully carved a significant market share for its super premium brand, the threat from competing products is ever present. **Table 2.1** presents the main competitors with which Java Republic competes across its target market segments. In addition to this, Java Republic also faces growing competition from own label coffee products. These products benefit retailers via substantially lower wholesale prices, resulting in a situation where the supermarkets' margins on the generics are higher than on branded goods. As indicated earlier, Java Republic has responded to this demand for own label products by producing a range of blends for private label. Already, Java Republic has developed a private label for the Superquinn chain.

Increased competition in recent years has also emerged from the popularity of Nespresso. To drink Nespresso coffee, the customer must first purchase a machine equipped to prepare the coffee, which comes in a hermetically-sealed capsule. Nespresso augments the product offering with a dedicated club that offers personalised services and advice on how to create the ultimate coffee experience. In addition to this, Nespresso boutiques can be found in exclusive locations where customers can experience the coffee and purchase the capsules for home. Outside of these boutiques, customers can only purchase the coffee capsules online. The combination of the machine, the capsule, the club and the boutiques result in a brand that is highly differentiated and unique in the market. The necessity to have a machine suited to the capsule could signal a change in the nature of competition in the coffee market going forward. This is a development that David is keenly watching, in particular given that Nespresso is increasingly focused on the food service segment of the market, where previously its attentions were focused on the 'at home' coffee-drinking segment of the market.

Table 2.1: Java Republic's Competitors

Competition	Description
Bewley's	The Bewley's name is one of Ireland's most recognised and trusted brands of ground coffee in Ireland. With 92% brand awareness in Ireland and recognised as a supplier of premium teas and coffees, the company has been at the centre of the country's coffee and tea industries since 1840.
Kraft Foods – Kenco, Maxwell House, Carte Noire	Kenco uses the same high quality Arabica beans in its instant as it does in its Roast and Ground coffee – according to the company, this is so that consumers can enjoy a delicious freeze-dried coffee in an instant. Maxwell House is a brand leader in the coffee powder sector, with 50g, 100g, 200g and 300g sizes. Maxwell House is also available in cappuccino format, with three variants to choose from: Cappuccino, Unsweetened Cappuccino and Latte. Carte Noire is available in three varieties: Carte Noire Instant Coffee, Carte Noire Decaffeinated and Carte Noire Ground Coffee. It has a very distinct packaging of black and gold and uses Arabica beans.
Robert Roberts	The company known today as Robert Roberts Ltd encompasses a range of traditional Irish companies engaged in the food and drinks markets. It specialises in premium coffees that are 100% Arabica. Each pack has a special valve on the back to ensure maximum freshness.

Competition	Description
Illy	The Illy brand is produced in Trieste, Italy. Illy produces only one blend of 100% Arabica coffee in three roast variations: normal, dark roast or decaffeinated. The blend is packaged as beans (yet to be ground), pre-ground coffee or E.S.E. pods. Illy sells to three segments: bars and hotels and restaurants, homes via stores and supermarkets, and offices via agents and distributors.
Rombouts	Rombouts is a family-owned coffee-making company, based in Belgium, with a total sales turnover of €120 million. Rombouts offers a full product line of coffee, including ground and whole bean coffee, espresso pods, pads and filters.
Lavazza	Lavazza is an Italian manufacturer of coffee products. Branded as 'Italy's Favourite Coffee', the company reports that 16 out of the 20 million coffee-purchasing families in Italy choose Lavazza. Among its many offerings today are products such as Top Class, Super Crema, Grand'Espresso, and Dek (decaffeinated).
Green Bean	Green Bean Coffee Roasters is an Irish speciality coffee roaster, with facilities in Co. Louth and Newry. Only Arabica beans are used by Green Bean Coffee Roasters.
Nescafé	According to Nestlé, Nescafé is the world's No.1 coffee brand in the market. The company maintains that over 300 million cups of Nescafé and other Nestlé soluble coffees are consumed everyday. Nescafé is the No.1 manufacturer with a 46.9% value share (AC Nielsen) of the €44 million Irish soluble coffee market.
Cafédirect	Cafédirect is the only 100% fair-trade brand available in Ireland and one of the world's largest 100% fair-trade hot drinks companies. It claims to offer the Irish consumer great-tasting products whilst enhancing the quality of life in the communities who produce the coffee, tea and cocoa. Cafédirect's 100% fair-trade range includes Cafédirect Roast and Ground coffee, 5065 Freeze dried coffee, Teadirect and Cocodirect (drinking chocolate).
Douwe Egberts	Douwe Egberts (a Dutch corporation) has been perfecting the art of making coffee for almost 250 years. Douwe Egberts Real Coffee is available in filter or cafetière blends. It comes in 250g and 500g packs in three flavours, with varying strengths: mild, medium and strong.
Cork Coffee Roasters	Cork Coffee Roasters is a Cork city-based, owner-operated, gourmet coffee company, specialising in small-batch coffee roasting and espresso preparation, and espresso equipment. All its coffees are handroasted, blended to order, delivered and shipped within 24 hours.

LEADING THE BRAND

David is a firm believer that a company's greatest asset is its people. He adopted the culture from day one, that by implementing a strong, well-rounded management team, in turn they will build teams of individuals around them that will foster a positive working attitude for company expansion, which will assist in scaling up Java Republic from a small enterprise to a medium-sized operation. Java Republic is managed by an experienced team, led by Grace O'Shaughnessy, who reports directly to David McKernan. **Figure 2.2** presents Java Republic's Organisational Structure.

Figure 2.2: Java Republic's Organisational Structure

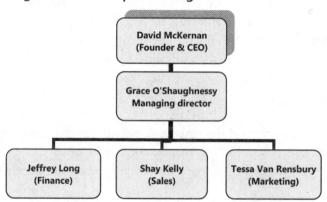

The management team meets once a month to discuss and evaluate the progress in each department. On a company-wide level, Java Republic holds a monthly staff meeting, where all employees, including the CEO, meet to discuss in an open forum issues ranging from whether to brand the top of the roof of the company's vans to who is responsible for keeping the canteen clean. The principle is that each member of staff has something valid to say. This also ensures that there isn't a 'them *versus* us' attitude, which can create unnecessary dissension in the workplace.

David has said that "our employees are dedicated, motivated and believe in our vision and mission: they are passionate about coffee". The working environment in Java Republic is fun, hardworking and fair with complete focus on product quality and strong customer relationships. In reflection of this culture, its staff turnover is consistently low – a thorough recruitment process assesses the behavioural characteristics of potential employees.

McKernan believes that employees need to be engaged in the future of the company at every opportunity in order to build and maintain organisational strength and to instil a sense of pride, productivity and fulfilment. Java Republic has operated from its inception a work environment of trust and staff have a mutual respect for each other. Rather than dictate deadlines or working hours or constant face-time, the department manager and the management team work with each employee to get the best from them. David understands the importance of the CEO in creating the company's culture: "You can market to death but the bottom line is that you've got to be true to what you're talking about. It comes from the top. If you don't believe in it, it will never fizzle down to the people around you. You've got to believe you're making great coffee and, if you've got a bunch of like-minded people, then it just makes it a little easier to grow your business".

While Java Republic does not operate a written work/life balance policy, it has adopted a culture focused on ensuring a positive balance for employees. Employees enjoy a longer holiday period than most; from the beginning, employees have been free to take in excess of the standard two-week summer break and are encouraged to travel to other continents. However, in line with the economic climate, this offering is now assessed on a one-to-one basis. More recently, the company introduced 'Company Days' – where Good Friday and Christmas Eve are given to staff as a thank you for their work throughout the year.

David believes that investing in staff will result in an additional unique selling point for the company as it ensures that it will use the capabilities of its people to their full potential and therefore allow the company to maintain a competitive edge in the market place.

GROWING THE BRAND

When Java Republic entered the market, the customer base was divided into two segments: Food Service and Retail and Online sales. In 2009, however, it noticed a trend towards going for a 'decent coffee and a cigarette' whilst in the office and as a result began to actively target the Coffee@Work segment (Office Coffee Accounts). Java Republic currently has an estimated 12% market share of the Food Service and Coffee at Work industry. Java Republic's focus has primarily been on the food service market in Ireland, with 96% of its turnover resulting from sales to restaurants, cafés, hotels, coffee houses, offices and corporate catering around the country. The retail and online market accounts for the remaining 4% of turnover.

While Java Republic's core product is coffee, its product range extends to hot chocolate and a wide variety of teas. In addition, Java Republic offers a range of coffee equipment, accessories and cookies. To the foodservice market, Java Republic supplements the above by offering the latest and most innovative coffee-brewing equipment and providing extensive barista training on-site. **Table 2.2** below presents a brief overview of Java Republic's products and the relevant target markets.

Table 2.2: Java Republic's Product Range

Product	Market Segment			
	Food Service	Retail	Online Sales	Coffee@Work
Coffee	√	√	√	√
Tea	√		√	√
Hot Chocolate	√		√	
Machinery/Accessories	√		√	

Java Republic's coffee range includes organic, fair-trade and decaffeinated products and includes a range of coffee beans and ground coffee for either filter or plunger in medium, dark strength or extra dark strength roasts. An advantage Java Republic has over competitors is that it is the only roaster that still makes specific grinds for both plunger and filter coffee machines.

Responding to research by Nielsen in 2009 which showed that private label (own label) coffee sales had gained market share in 14 out of 20 European countries and actually holds 30% market share in 10 of these countries, Java Republic made the decision to handroast custom blends for key foodservice and retail customers. These bespoke coffees offer the foodservice clients unique control over quality and pricing without sacrificing any of Java Republic's quality standards. Superquinn became the first company to agree a deal with Java Republic for private label coffee.

The real leaf tea range includes speciality, fair-trade and organic loose teas, which are designed to complement the premium coffee offering. The traditional brew is a single origin Kenyan tea, while the speciality teas range from wild berry infusion to blood orange. These teas are packed in a hand-sewn silken teabag, each one sealed for flavour in its own foil pouch. The organic loose tea range explores the natural flavours of traditional black tea, Chinese green tea, rare white tea and refreshing fruit infusions. The hot chocolate product, named "The Other Bean" is differentiated from other brands by its 40% cocoa content and its dash of cane sugar sourced from a fair-trade co-op in Malawi. The product is designed to appeal to a food purist and to the tastes of the average chocoholic.

Since the company's inception in 1999, it has won more than 94 medals at the Great Taste Awards, which are considered the Oscars of the fine food world. The latest scoop of medals in 2009 totalled 7 and is a reflection of the quality of the company's products.

In targeting the food service segment, the company uses a business model based on direct relationship selling through their sales team – seeing their customers as 'partners'. The sales team comprises sales area managers and regional distributors. Java Republic has five distributors that service the food service territories outside Dublin, (namely Munster, East Midlands, West, North East and South East) and two area sales representatives who manage the Dublin area. The retail segment is serviced by Stafford Lynch, the company's national retail distributors.

To build relationships with corporate customers, the trade is encouraged to visit Java Republic and experience the ritual of the roasting process and the cupping of freshly-made coffee, teas and hot chocolate. Each corporate customer must commit to engage in an educational programme where they receive the skills required to be a barista. To maintain this relationship, clients are serviced by a team of Java engineers who are trained to install and fix coffee machines and equipment. This service department runs 24 hours, 364 days a year. In attempting to grow the food service segment, marketing director Tessa Van Rensbury or other Java Republic employees regularly attend both national and international trade shows. However, while they have found these to be effective from a PR and branding perspective, they are less so in recruiting customers; the sales team are generally regarded as the most effective at this.

In targeting both the corporate and customer segments, the company uses a combination of public relations and below the line promotional activities to differentiate its brand from that of competitors. On entering the market initially, much of the company's promotion centred on building the brand through public relations (see **Appendix 2**). Promotional literature was designed to be engaging, educational and comparative, with David leading the communication policy of the company. Over time, the company's promotion has evolved into a strategy focused on increasing the brand presence and reinforcing the image of an ethically-produced super premium brand.

The product's packaging has been central to the success of the brand, winning the Packaging Category of the Year at the Irish Design Effectiveness

Awards in 2000. The packaging is bright yellow, featuring imagery from the Aztec Empire (see **Appendix 3**). This distinctive packaging ensures that the brand commands a strong presence and thus works to create awareness and a distinctive image for the brand in the mind of the consumer. In building the brand's reputation as a super premium brand, much promotional literature focuses on the quality establishments such as L'Ecrivain restaurant in Dublin's city centre and the Sheen Falls Hotel, Kenmare, County Kerry, which serve Java Republic products. Carefully-planned complementary promotional campaigns with brands such as Baileys and Bodum further maintain the image of a unique exclusive brand.

While Java Republic has not had the finance to invest in large scale advertising and promotion of the brand, a low cost method of communicating the company's ethos and image does exist in an online environment. The Java Republic website was originally designed to be thought-provoking, challenging and personal, and to be uniquely different from that of most other commercial organisations. Driving customers to the website, however, has proved problematic. To address this issue, Tessa Van Rensbury has engaged in a complete redesign of the website and has embraced the potential of social media, such as Facebook, to actively communicate with customers and potential customers. It is probable, however, that engagement in traditional communications methods combined with an online presence will be required if Java Republic is to grow its retail market segment.

The premium policy of the company is central to the brand image of a high quality differentiated brand. Java Republic coffee is approximately 20% more expensive than the market leader and is the most expensive coffee in the world next to Illy. Tea and hot chocolate are available to purchase online and are also sold to food service; however, they are not available to purchase in retail outlets. In keeping with the coffee pricing structure, these products are sold at a price premium.

An increasingly difficult trading environment in recent years, however, has forced Java Republic to reassess its pricing structure and to work to retain customers by discussing pricing on a one-to-one basis. This has resulted in a pro-active pricing strategy where some price discounting is offered to customers, along with the provision of free stock to attain a competitive edge in the market place. Despite these increased pricing pressures, Java Republic prefers to focus on education and the creation of value in customer's outlets to creatively address the pricing demands. For example, by focusing on aspects such as cup size, using crockery *versus* disposable cups, reducing wastage through adherence to proper machine settings, etc, Java Republic has identified where customers can save costs in areas other than price reductions. On average, Java Republic's gross margin is between 49% and 52%.

On entering the retail market in 2005, the product was at a 47% premium price to the market leader, at €6.29 across the product range. However, increased price competition in retail has resulted in a price reduction across the product range to a price of €4.29 for filter and plunger and €4.59 for beans. At this price, Java Republic coffee is still at a price premium but the company is concerned that the nature of competition in the market is increasingly price-oriented; Java prefers to focus on education and marketing to support the image of a super premium brand, and has little desire to engage in further price discounting. Careful pricing policy remains central to Java's brand management plan over the next three years.

The management team is aware that there exists a strong need to grow the retail segment of the market, which currently accounts for only 4% of their turnover, and the type of promotional activity that they have engaged in to date has had little impact on this segment. Competition in this market is price-based and Java Republic is unwilling to engage in a promotional strategy that is based on price. To grow the brand in this segment, significant investment is required to educate the customer about the Java Republic brand, its ethics and its premium Irish position; at present, however, the company does not have the money to do this. Outside investment, or a significant increase in its share of the food service segment, could yield the money required to grow this segment.

TIME TO MAKE SOME DECISIONS

With David marooned in Toronto, the management team convenes for its monthly meeting. As always, various issues are up for discussion, including mounting competition, stretched financing, branding issues, managing productivity/capacity, managing growth, etc. However, dominating the agenda are capacity and cost/pricing issues.

Currently, Java Republic is only operating at 20% of its potential production capacity – a situation that cannot continue indefinitely. Expanding the customer base into the North of Ireland and the UK is a possibility, as is further expansion across Europe. There also exists the opportunity to expand production of private label coffee; however, Tessa has reservations that this might result in cannibalising the Java Republic brand. Her preference is to grow the brand in the retail market but this requires investment that the company is currently lacking.

The current volatile market means that 'price, price, price' is on the top of everyone's list. In the last year, finance director Jeffrey Long has worked pro-actively to cut back on costs and to creatively solve the issue of price by offering the customer value and creating value in their outlets. However, the continuing recession means that cost and pricing pressures are relentless. Balancing these pressures with the necessity to retain customers and maintain the brand image is challenging.

Meanwhile, back in Toronto, David is also thinking about the production capacity problems. His trip to Toronto inspired thoughts about franchising the roastery house concept internationally, and thinking beyond the UK and Europe. David ponders the possibility of supplying the North American and Canadian coffee market.

Finally, David is also grappling with a personal dilemma that not all members of his team are aware of. Java Republic has been approached recently as an acquisition target by a large coffee company. Would this be the right time for David to exit the market? On a personal level, this decision would offer David a well-deserved break from his hectic lifestyle and true financial freedom. The unexpected flight delay in Toronto has left David with much time to consider these issues. It is clear that a lot of tough decisions have to be made for the Java Republic brand.

QUESTIONS

1. What are Java Republic's distinctive competencies? What are some of the challenges in maintaining these competencies?

2. Outline the key brand management issues for Java Republic for the next three years.

3. Expand on the characteristics of David's entrepreneurial spirit and discuss the impact that these traits have had on the success of the company.

4. As a member of the management team, what future strategy do you see as most appropriate for the company in its current position?

APPENDIX 1: THE ROASTERY AND COFFEE HOUSE

APPENDIX 2: PR STRATEGY

Don't abuse the bean

● 'Fresh, unusual blends, with a focused lightness' — David McKernan, managing director of Java Republic, with coffee roaster, Paul Mooney, right.
Photograph:Dara Mac Dónaill

Coffee and Praline Charlotte

For the charlotte
50 g (2oz) ground coffee
600 ml (1 pint) milk
5 egg yolks
100g (4oz) caster sugar
11g (scant half oz) leaf gelatine, soaked, or one sachet gelatine powder
450 ml (¾ pint) cream
24 sponge finger biscuits
2 tablespoons Tia Maria
2 tablespoons water, in which you have dissolved one level teaspoon sugar

For the praline
50 grams (2oz) hazelnuts
50g (2oz) caster sugar

● Java Republic, The Roastery, Citylink Business park, Old Naas Road, Dublin 12. Tel: 01-4563306. Email: mailorder@java-republic.com. Java Republic coffees are widely available.
● Food Solutions, Seafield Road, Blackrock, Co Louth. Tel: 042-9323922

Stripping down to bare essentials

By Jennifer O'Connell

S mooth, wholesome and totally pure — and that's only the coffee. The brothers behind the Java Republic coffee company and staff at Nude Restaurants stripped to the bare essentials last week for the launch of Blue Earth, Ireland's first hand-roasted organic coffee.

Developed especially for Nude, which is to open its second branch on Leeson Street in Dublin on Thursday, the coffee is made from organically-grown beans imported from Mexico, Guatemala and Peru.

"Coffee is one of the most chemically-treated crops — it's second only to tobacco and just ahead of cotton," says David McKernan, founder of Java Republic.

One year ago, Java Republic — which was set up by McKernan who had spent the previous 12 years at Bewleys — was processing its first order for one crate of coffee beans.

Today, it controls 11 per cent of the catering market, with more than 240 wholesale clients.

It plans to begin distributing its grade one coffee to retail outlets in the next few months.

The Blue Earth organic fair-trade mark coffee, which takes 70 minutes to roast by hand (the industry norm is eight minutes), will be served initially to diners in Nude's two Dublin restaurants.

David McKernan, Java, David Quirke, Nude, Philip McKernan, Java, and Gerard Forde, Nude   GARY O'NEILL

APPENDIX 3: PACKAGING

3

PHONES MADE EASY

Aisling Conway and Michael Walsh

CASE SYNOPSIS

Two brothers Rowland and Damien Lenihan, opened a mobile phone retail business in Kilmallock, Co Limerick, in November 2008. Target segments were individual customers for mobile phones and broadband, and SMEs in south Limerick and North Cork. The case outlines the entrepreneurs' background and their motivation for starting a new business. It traces the launch and development of the business over its first 18 months. The new business encountered challenges during its first year, such as a decision by O_2 to discontinue the agency which was the backbone of Phones Made Easy's business. Rowland and Damien managed to secure an alternative dealership for 3 mobile phones and broadband. The business suffered cashflow problems, accentuated by changes in the phone suppliers they deal with. While trading through a credit squeeze and the recession, Phones Made Easy did well to get placed in the top five retailers in Ireland of 3 mobile phones and broadband, in December 2009.

As banks were unwilling to advance further loans to Phones Made Easy, the owners had recourse to family and friends to provide additional finance that was necessary to operate the business. The Lenihan brothers have impressed 3 so much, that 3 offered them the opportunity of opening one of 20 franchised mobile phone stores, planned by 3 nationally. Rowland and Damien must now assess the viability of a new 3 franchise store in a busy Limerick city shopping centre, and choose a strategic path for Phones Made Easy over the coming three years.

INTRODUCTION

As they shut their mobile phone and broadband store in Kilmallock, Co. Limerick, on Saturday evening of the May holiday weekend 2010, brothers Rowland and Damien Lenihan reflected on 18 eventful months' trading. Their mobile phone retail business, Phones Made Easy, had come through a deepening recession, a credit squeeze, cashflow problems, and significant changes in their dealership contracts. Despite such challenges and a loss of €3,000 in its first year, Phones Made Easy had been trading well in recent months and stood on the brink of a major expansion opportunity.

The Lenihan brothers had opened a new mobile phone and broadband business in Kilmallock in November 2008, as Ireland was entering a recession. They had little difficulty getting set-up finance of €10,000 from Bank of Ireland. Although the first 12 months' trading did not produce any profit, by

Christmas 2009, Phones Made Easy was one of the top five retail stores in Ireland selling 3 mobile phone and broadband products. This earned Damien an all-expenses-paid trip to Hong Kong, home of Hutchison Whampoa Limited (HWL), parent of 3 mobile. Phones Made Easy was recently approached by 3 to set up a 3 franchise store in a popular shopping centre in Limerick city. This new store would require further finance, and staff would need to be recruited. Determined to make a success of their business, Rowland and Damien had scheduled most of the holiday weekend to assess their options, and examine the implications of the expansion offer from 3.

BACKGROUND OF THE ENTREPRENEURS

Brothers Rowland and Damien Lenihan grew up near the Cork border town of Charleville, in Cregane, Co. Limerick.

Damien graduated from University College Cork (UCC) in 2004 with a BA (Economics and Maths), and completed a Higher Diploma in Health Economics at UCC in 2005. Following graduation, he took a position with health insurer BUPA Ireland in Fermoy, Co. Cork, where he worked as a Customer Service Advisor for 15 months, and a Customer Service Team Leader for 9 months. According to Damien, "I learned how to deal with the public and any problems they may have. I learned organisational skills, such as how to lead people, how to work out rotas, how to discipline people, how to chair meetings and to deal with staff issues". Damien then joined Citco Fund Services in Cork city as a Fund Accountant. He describes this as "a more analytical role, working on financial statements for a fund of hedge funds for long days and to very strict guidelines". With this education and experience, Damien took the role of financial director of Phones Made Easy with responsibility for ordering stock and dealing with day-to-day finances.

Rowland Lenihan, the elder brother, graduated with a Certificate in Music Management and Sound Engineering from Coláiste Stiofáin Naofa, Cork, in 1998. His first job was with phone retailer Lets Talk Phones, where he served as assistant manager in the company's main retail outlet on Patrick Street, Cork city. The Lets Talk Phones retail chain was later purchased by Eircell, and became part of Vodafone, with its takeover of Eircell in 2001. Shortly afterwards, he was promoted to manager of Vodafone's flagship store on Oliver Plunkett Street, Cork city. In 2006, Rowland changed jobs to become a Business Development Manager for O_2. This was a high pressure role in business-to-business (B2B) sales, with specific targets to meet every month. He worked for two and a half years in this position before setting up Phones

Made Easy with his brother, where he took the role of sales director due to his sales experience in the industry.

The brothers share the duties of managing the store, and each goes on the road to visit prospective business customers.

OPPORTUNITY BECKONS

The brothers were unhappy in their PAYE roles, and had a desire to own and manage their own business. According to Rowland, "I always had the ambition to be self-employed and, after working in the phone industry for 11 years, it was time to take the chance on doing it for myself". The brothers were brought up in a self-employed environment: their father operates an electrical contracting business with his eldest son. With Rowland's strong background in the mobile phone industry, they decided to set up their own retail outlet – Phones Made Easy. Damien understood that "mobile phones are not just used as phones any longer. They are now internet devices, music players, cameras, organisers etc. They are not a product that is going away, so I suppose there is safety in the industry". Annual mobile phone revenue in Ireland was €1.7 billion in 2009 (www.comreg.ie).

They chose Kilmallock as a location for a mobile phone shop, as there was no mobile phone outlet in the town or elsewhere in south Co. Limerick. The store would also service the surrounding areas of Bruree, Effin, Kilfinane and Bruff. Kilmallock, with a population of 1,443 (www.cso.ie), has had some positive developments in recent times. Limerick County Council opened a new €6 million Area Office, Regional Library and Courthouse in Kilmallock on 23 November 2009. A new €800,000 community enterprise centre is currently under construction; due for completion in December 2010, it should be open in the coming months. The centre will provide space for small enterprises and new start-ups in Kilmallock and the South Limerick area and also will have a link with third-level institutions. Street surfaces and pavements have been renewed in recent years, adding to its attractiveness for shoppers. Kilmallock livestock mart is a big draw every Monday for farmers from surrounding areas, as it is the only mart in the south Limerick area.

The nearest mobile phone retail competitor is five miles away in Charleville, Co. Cork. Location is very important in obtaining a dealership.[1] With no mobile phone store in south Limerick, and with Rowland's connections in O_2, Phones Made Easy was granted an O_2 dealership. In

---

[1] An agency from a mobile phone network to sell their product.

January 2009, Phones Made Easy also obtained a dealership to sell Meteor pre-pay phones.

South Cork County Enterprise Board (CEB) provided advice on writing the business plan. As a retail business and, at that time, not creating employment beyond the jobs of the two founder-owners, Phones Made Easy was not entitled to grant assistance from the CEB.

IRISH MOBILE PHONE COMPETITORS

There are five mobile phone providers in Ireland: O_2, Vodafone, Meteor, Tesco mobile and **3**. The Commission for Communications Regulation (Comreg) is the statutory body for regulation of the telecommunications sector in Ireland. A recent (2009) Comreg report on the mobile and broadband communications market shows that Vodafone has 39% market share, O_2 has 33%, Meteor has 19.8% and **3** has 8.2% of the overall market (Tesco mobile was not included in the study). **Figure 3.1** illustrates the four mobile phone providers' market shares.

Figure 3.1: Market Share of Mobile Phone Subscriptions, 2007-2009

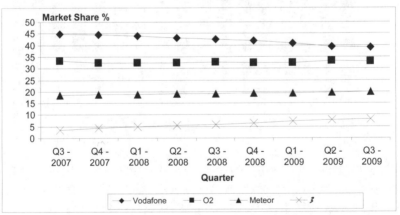

Source: Comreg Quarterly Key Data Report (Q3-2009).

Tesco mobile and **3** are the latest entrants to the Irish mobile phone market. **3** (the trading name of Hutchison 3G Ireland) was awarded a mobile phone licence by the Irish government in June 2002. Its parent, Hutchison Whampoa Limited, is an international corporation based in Hong Kong with businesses in retailing, property development, infrastructure, port facilities and telecommunications (www.hutchison-whampoa.com). Tesco mobile was awarded a mobile licence in October 2007. Comreg reports that quarterly revenue for the Irish mobile phone industry in Q3-2009 was €445,549,041. There are approximately five million mobile phones in use in Ireland, whose population is approximately 4.2 million (www.irishlinks.co.uk).

Figure 3.2 demonstrates that Ireland has a 117.3% mobile penetration rate, whereas the EU average is 125.5%. Greece has the highest mobile phone penetration rate of 180%.

Figure 3.2: European Mobile Penetration Rates

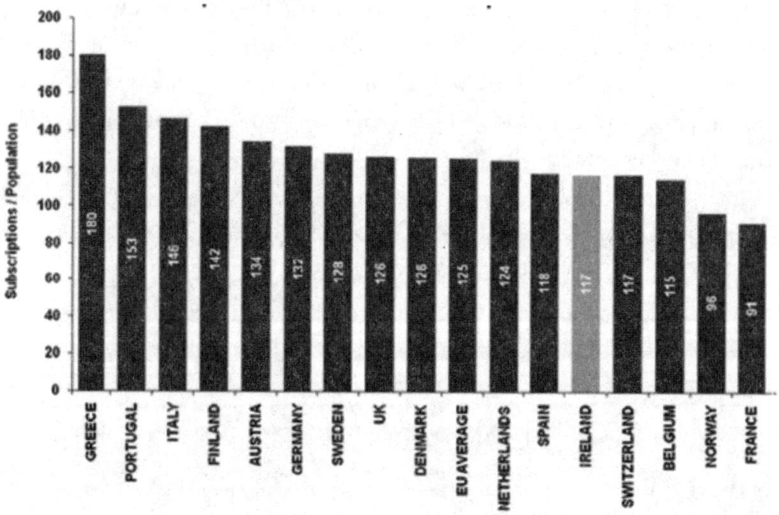

Source: Comreg Quarterly Key Data Report (Q3-2009)

While these data indicate some scope for Ireland's mobile phone ownership rate to rise to the EU average, growth in mobile phone revenues is expected to come from two main sources. First, sales of upgraded phones as new models with new technology features are launched. In April 2010, the German government was expected to raise between €5 billion and €10 billion from auctioning the 4G (4th Generation) mobile phone network licence, the first government in Europe to do so (www.bbc.co.uk). The 4G mobile phone will have internet connection up to 10 times faster than 3G mobile phones. This will enable users of 4G mobiles to watch TV broadcasts and download online games. The second source of revenue growth is additional mobile contract and

top-up charges, as users run more video games and internet applications on
their phones.

THE 3 NETWORK

3 holds fourth position in terms of mobile market share in Ireland but it is
making huge strides in the mobile broadband sector. "3 is the market leader in
mobile broadband with over 200,000 mobile broadband subscribers in Ireland
and 4.5 million worldwide" (www.three.ie). 3 was the first network in Ireland
to offer mobile broadband with a datacard modem, and was first with a pre-
pay mobile broadband service. 3 boasts a high speed network of 7.2 Mb per
second and it plans to double this speed by the end of 2010. 3 has been
innovative in pricing of mobile phone services; it was the first company in
Ireland to offer customers a price plan combining pre-pay and bill-pay known
as the 'best of both'. This price plan is a fixed bill amount of €15, €25 or €45 a
month and customers have the flexibility of topping up if they exceed their bill
amount. 3 was also the first mobile phone network to offer Windows Live
Messenger. Along with mobile phone providers Vodafone and O₂, 3 will offer
the iPhone 4 for purchase from July 2010. 3 is a dynamic, fast-growing network
and is promoting its brand through sponsorship of the Ian Dempsey Breakfast
Show (Today FM), the Irish Golf Open in 2009 and 2010, the Irish Soccer
team, Waterford GAA, Waterford United and UL Bohemians (www.three.ie).

COMPANY VISION

First, the Lenihans had to decide whether to form a limited company, or
operate as a sole trader or a partnership. They decided on the latter, at the
request of the bank. If the business did not succeed, the bank believed it
would be easier to recover money from the individuals rather than from a
limited company. The company targeted retail and business sales. The store in
Kilmallock would sell mobile phones, mobile broadband, mobile phone
accessories and small electronic products such as Apple iPods and car kits.
Business sales focused on providing mobile phone services to small and
medium enterprises and professionals in south Limerick and north Cork
regions. The company's mission statement is to be a "leader in quality, price
and service in the sale of mobile phones".

Phones Made Easy set the following targets for year one:

1. Become established in the locality and build a reputation as a centre of excellence in the provision of mobile phones and mobile broadband.
2. To make a small profit, thereby building equity in the business.
3. To begin establishing the Phones Made Easy brand throughout the south Limerick/north Cork regions.

Damien believes they have achieved target one and have partially delivered on target three. They believe two years of hard work are needed in sales, service and promoting the business in order to achieve target two.

From an economics point of view, Phones Made Easy holds a local monopoly; it is the only firm in Kilmallock that sells mobile phones. However, the broader Irish mobile phone market has a monopolistically competitive market structure (Turley, Maloney and O'Toole, 2006:175). The market is characterised by a large number of retail outlets, which compete on product quality, price and marketing.

From the beginning, Phones Made Easy marketed only O_2 phone products. In January 2009, it was appointed agents for Meteor network mobile phones, so it sought to gain from the reputation of O_2 and Meteor, while building recognition and support for the Phones Made Easy brand. Competition in the mobile phones and broadband market is based on product innovation – for example, iPhone, 4G mobile, brand advertising and sponsorship, competitive price bundles, and service level and expertise of retail sales outlets.

COMPANY FINANCES

The key costs of the business can be broken into three areas: once-off set-up costs, recurring fixed costs and variable costs. The costs of set-up totalled approximately €12,000. This included flooring, suspended ceiling, paint, counters, office desk, cash register, two laptops, a computer and printer. Fixed costs are constant for the business, and are independent of sales volume. They include, for example, rent (€100 per week), rates (€842 per year) and insurance (€600 per year). Variable costs are dependent on the level of sales: the more the company sells, the higher the variable costs. Variable costs for the company include telephone, internet, light and heat, advertising and wages.

The owners had a small amount of money to invest in setting up the business, and they approached the bank for the remainder. They prepared a detailed business plan, and had it reviewed by an accountant. The bank was impressed with their business plan, and the €5,000 'hurt money' Rowland and Damien were willing to invest. 'Hurt money' is money that owners are willing to put at risk in a business, and without this the bank may not have granted the loan. From the bank's point of view, the owners had a good mix of skills and knowledge to make the business a success. The bank advanced €10,000 for repayment over five years. Repayments are made monthly, at 7% interest on the reducing balance.

With the finance sanctioned, the brothers began internal work on the retail unit, and created a small office and store room at the back of the store. One regret Phones Made Easy has is not asking the bank for more finance at the outset, as they had no difficulty in getting set-up finance. Getting further finance since the shop opened has been a huge difficulty.

THE LAUNCH

Phones Made Easy began trading on 3 November 2008, a month later than planned. The opening was delayed as they were waiting for phone lines, the O_2 dealership papers took longer than expected, and internal work on the shop contributed to the delay. Rowland states, "This was an inexperience issue, one which I would hope to rectify if I were doing it again". The opening of the store was low-key and, in retrospect, the owners feel they should have got a well-known personality to open the store, in order to raise its profile from the start. **Table 3.1** details the main products sold by Phones Made Easy in its early months.

Table 3.1: Phones Made Easy's Product Range at Start-up

O_2 (from Nov 2008)	Meteor (from Jan 2009)
Pre - Pay Mobile Phones	Pre – Pay Mobile Phones
Bill - Pay Mobile Phones	
Broadband (Contract)	

During the first weeks of trading, Phones Made Easy took a centre page advertisement in the local newspaper, the *Vale Star*. This included photos and profiles of the owners, interior and exterior of the shop, and products for sale. They did a number of flyer drops in housing estates in the town and surrounding areas. Phones Made Easy has used newspaper advertising to increase sales of contract products with moderate results. Flyers have proven to be a more successful marketing instrument than newspaper advertising, with customers bringing in flyers to avail of special offers.

Phones Made Easy joined Business Networking Ireland (BNI) in May 2009 for an annual fee of €870, as another method of creating sales. In BNI, small and medium enterprises (SMEs) learn about each other's business. Members attend weekly breakfast meetings with the purpose of creating business for each other. Phones Made Easy joined two BNI chapters: in Limerick city, attended by Rowland, and Mallow, Co. Cork, attended by Damien. Phones Made Easy pays an annual membership fee to each chapter, and has found this marketing method moderately successful.

DIFFICULTIES ENCOUNTERED SINCE LAUNCH

Phones Made Easy has encountered a number of challenges since start-up.

Financial Difficulties

The Lenihan brothers approached the bank since start-up to ask for an overdraft and additional finance for a company van. They have been turned down on two occasions. According to Damien, "further finance or even an overdraft from the bank is impossible to get". The company considered moving their business to another bank, but they found banks are unwilling to lend to them at the moment. Mazars, an independent Irish consultancy firm, published a review of bank lending to SMEs between October 2009 and December 2009. They found a 20% decline in lending to SMEs, and one in five SMEs was not getting enough credit. Mazars concluded that this could lead to business closures and loss of jobs (www.sfa.ie). The Minister of Finance set up the Credit Review Office in March 2010. SMEs can apply to the Credit Review Office for a review of a loan application that has been turned down by a financial institution (www.finance.gov.ie). Provided it is satisfied with the merits of the loan application, the Credit Review Office will approach the financial institution on the SME's behalf, for a nominal fee (www.creditreview.ie). This is an avenue that Phones Made Easy may yet explore.

The company has encountered cashflow problems. Mobile phone retailing has an appetite for working capital. Stock is bought and paid for initially by the retailer. Commissions are not paid until the mobile phones have been sold. Thus, there can be a time lag, depending on how quickly the stock is sold. One can see that an overdraft facility is of vital significance for the company. An Irish Central Bank review (January 2010) of lending to the business sector confirms Mazars' appraisal. It found that the wholesale, retail trade and repairs sector endured a decrease of 10.6% in lending in 2009 (www.centralbank.ie). Following refusal by the bank, Phones Made Easy has received financial support from family and friends.

O$_2$ Changes its Distribution Policy

Phones Made Easy's contract with O$_2$ gave it a licence to sell O$_2$ mobile phones. It secured the dealership relatively easily, as Rowland had connections with O$_2$ and a successful track record in the phones business. However, in July 2009, O$_2$ decided to change its trading policy. O$_2$ mobile phones would now be sold through O$_2$ franchise retail stores and Carphone Warehouse and would no longer be sold through independent dealers such as Phones Made Easy. This was a huge blow, as the company had built up relationships with O$_2$ business and private customers, and O$_2$ mobile was their main product. Phones Made Easy had a decision to make: should it cease trading and cut their losses, or refinance the business, and tie in with another network such as **3**. Vodafone was not a possibility; there is a Vodafone dealer in Charleville, just five miles from Kilmallock. This was a difficult decision, particularly as further bank credit was not forthcoming. However, family and friends of the owners refinanced Phones Made Easy, enabling it to continue trading with **3** and Meteor as suppliers. According to Rowland, "The withdrawal of O$_2$ hit the business extremely hard, and looked at the time that it would close us down. It took investment and support from family and friends to stay afloat". They quickly obtained a full dealership with **3**, which enables Phones Made Easy to sell to both business and private customers. It hopes to secure the rights to sell Meteor products to business customers in the near future.

During this difficult time, Phones Made Easy had a burglary in its Kilmallock premises. A small amount of cash and stock was taken. The insurance policy covered the losses, but it took a number of weeks for the insurance money to come through. In spite of these considerable setbacks, the brothers decided to continue trading and broaden their product base (see **Figure 3.2**). According to Damien, "After losing our O$_2$ dealership, we try to keep more power in our own hands and not in the hands of our suppliers, so that means building up our product base and not relying on one network".

Table 3.2: Phones Made Easy's Product Range from July 2009 to Present

3	Meteor	Sim-Free Phones
Pre-Pay Mobile Phones	Pre-Pay Mobile Phones	Pre-Pay Mobile Phones
Bill-Pay Mobile Phones		
Broadband – Contract		
Broadband – Pre-Pay		

New Supplier puts Pressure on Cashflow

Sigma Wireless was the distributor of *3* mobile phones to Phones Made Easy. Since the change over to the *3* network in July 2009, Phones Made Easy had developed a good working relationship with Sigma Wireless. Initially, commissions were paid on a monthly basis but, after some months, Sigma agreed to pay the commissions on a weekly basis. This helped to alleviate cashflow problems at Phones Made Easy. However, in January 2010, Sigma Wireless went into examinership, and ceased trading. Bright Point Ireland (BPI), on behalf of *3*, now supplies mobile phones to Phones Made Easy. This resulted in commissions once again being paid on a monthly basis, an unexpected additional stress on Phones Made Easy's cashflow. It was a setback for Damien and Rowland to have to develop a working relationship with a new supplier all over again.

Economic Climate

Since it opened in November 2008, the fledgling Phones Made Easy never experienced trading outside a recessionary period. Recent economic data, however, point to a better trading outlook. The Economic Social and Research Institute (ESRI) forecasts that Ireland's Gross Domestic Product (GDP) will grow by 2.5% in 2011. ESRI also expects the rate of unemployment and the general government deficit to decrease in 2011 (www.esri.ie). The Central Statistics Office Retail Sales Index was up 3 percentage points in February 2010 from February 2009, suggesting consumer confidence is rising (www.cso.ie). This is an encouraging trend for the two entrepreneurs.

MARKET OUTLOOK

Phones Made Easy had a difficult first year and, according to Damien, "we were lucky to keep our heads above water. Like any start-up, we hadn't foreseen making any profits in our first year". Phones Made Easy made a net loss of €3,000 in its first 12 months. The company's top-selling product is mobile broadband units. In 2008, **3** was awarded the contract to roll-out broadband throughout Ireland under the National Broadband Scheme. **3** is currently investing a substantial amount of money in developing its broadband network, and has plans to switch to 4G. According to Damien, "we should feel the knock-on effect of this on our sales".

As a result of the National Broadband Scheme, both **3** pre-pay and contract mobile broadband have been in high demand, particularly in rural areas, where broadband coverage had previously been poor. **3** enters a contract to provide broadband to customers for a 12-month period. The contract customer pays a fixed sum to **3** every month, for use of the broadband connection. For Phones Made Easy, a broadband contract is twice as profitable as a pre-pay customer for broadband. A bill-pay contract for a mobile phone on the other hand, is three times more profitable to Phones Made Easy than a customer purchasing a pre-pay phone. A pre-pay phone is where customers top up with credit according to their requirements, whereas a contract is a fixed bill amount every month. Sim-free phones have also been a popular product for the store. This is a phone that can be used on any network. This ensures that Phones Made Easy can also facilitate Vodafone and O_2 customers.

PROMOTION

In the past few months, the company redesigned its logo with the help of a Limerick-based graphic design company with the intention, in Rowland's words, "to look more professional". **Figure 3.3** illustrates the old logo and **Figure 3.4** illustrates the new Phones Made Easy logo following redesign.

Figure 3.3: Original Phones Made Easy Logo

[PHONES MADE EASY]

Phones Made Easy now operates a website (www.phonesmadeeasy.ie) with product information, contact details and special offers. It also re-designed its business cards and has a range of stationery bearing the new logo. Its first business card promoted the O_2 and Meteor networks, whose products it was selling at the beginning. The business card now features the Phones Made Easy brand only.

Figure 3.4: New Phones Made Easy Logo

CHALLENGES AHEAD

Phones Made Easy needs to be clear on its objectives and strategy for the medium term. The Lenihan brothers intend to build on their achievements in year one and further strengthen their brand. They feel a need to broaden their product mix, and are currently looking at selling computer products. Impressed by their hard work and success in establishing Phones Made Easy, **3** has approached them to open a franchise store that would trade under the **3** name. The store would be located in one of the main shopping centres in Limerick city, which has a weekly footfall of 40,000–60,000 people. The population of Limerick city in the 2006 census is 52,539 people, and its shopping catchment area expands this number considerably (www.cso.ie). Phones Made Easy would not have to pay for the franchise, and would receive financial assistance from **3** towards rent and marketing. **3** announced plans to open 28 retail stores around the country, creating 90 jobs in a €5 million investment. Eight of these stores will be owned by **3**, and 20 will be independently owned (www.three.ie). **3** selected the Lenihan brothers as possible owners of one of the 20 independent stores that will trade under the **3** brand name.

Excited by the prospect of opening their second store, the young entrepreneurs Rowland and Damien are aware of the challenges it would pose. They will need to raise additional capital and hire sales staff, at a time when credit has proved difficult to secure. An alternative route is to consolidate the Kilmallock unit over the coming two years, and to look for development options in 2012 when it is hoped that credit will be more readily available. Would an opportunity like a franchised phone store with 3 be available then? The brothers were resigned to long hours of discussion and financial estimation over the coming days as they weigh the options and plan a strategy for their company.

REFERENCES

Commission for Communications Regulation (Comreg) (2009). *Irish Communications Market, Quarterly Key Data Report Q3 2009*, Dublin: Comreg, available at http://www.comreg.ie/fileupload/publications/ ComReg09101.pdf, accessed 29 February 2010.

http://beyond2020.cso.ie/census/tableviewer/tableview.aspx?reportid=109360, accessed 20 April 2010.

http://beyond2020.cso.ie/Census/TableViewer/tableView.aspx?ReportId=75 467, accessed 13 May 2010.

http://centralbank.ie/data/MonthStatFiles/Dec%2009%20Note.pdf, accessed 13 April 2010.

http://news.bbc.co.uk/2/hi/business/8615465.stm, accessed 24 May 2010.

http://www.creditreview.ie/ReviewProcess_Apply.aspx, accessed 13 April 2010.

http://www.cso.ie/releasespublications/documents/services/current/rsi.pdf, accessed 26 April 2010.

http://www.esri.ie/news_events/latest_press_releases/quarterly_economic_co mmen_7/index.xm, accessed 26 April 2010.

http://www.finance.gov.ie/documents/publications/other/2010/Creditrevie woffice.pdf, accessed 13 April 2010.

http://www.hutchison-whampoa.com/europe/eng/global/home.htm, accessed 10 May 2010.

http://www.irishlinks.co.uk/mobile-phones-ireland.htm, accessed 7 January 2010.

http://www.sfa.ie/Sectors/SFA/SFA.nsf/vPages/Press_Centre~mazars-iii- report-on-lending-to-smes--sfa-comment-19-04-2010?OpenDocument, accessed 8 June 2010.

http://www.three.ie/about3/index.htm, accessed 13 September 2010.

http://www.three.ie/pdf/3Store%20Announcement%20comp.pdf, accessed 26 April 2010.

Turley, G., Maloney, M. and O'Toole, F. (2006). *Principle of Economics – An Irish Textbook*, Dublin: Gill and Macmillan.

QUESTIONS

1. Critically examine the start-up arrangements and marketing strategy adopted by Phones Made Easy.

2. Give your assessment of the first year's trading performance of Phones Made Easy.

3. Evaluate the offer to open a new **3** franchise store in a Limerick shopping centre in partnership with **3**.

4. If you were advising the Lenihan brothers as they prepare for their next meeting with **3**, what negotiating stance would you recommend? Explain your answer.

4

MCOR TECHNOLOGIES' MATRIX OF SUCCESS

Garrett Duffy

CASE SYNOPSIS

Mcor Technologies is a manufacturer of 3D printers based in Ardee, Co. Louth. Mcor has developed and patented its own range of printers to serve the modelling industry.

This case study covers the period from start-up to when Mcor Technologies secured first round venture capital funding. It outlines the entrepreneurial journey the company founders have undertaken. It focuses on the importance of planning and implementation at each stage of company development and also of widening the company's circle of advisors.

INTRODUCTION

Standing on the podium in the Ramada Hotel in Belfast with her husband Conor and brother-in-law Fintan, having just been announced as Inter*Trade*Ireland Seedcorn Competition overall winners (Best Emerging International Category), Deirdre MacCormack began to realise that people were starting to believe in Mcor Technologies – people other than the MacCormacks themselves. She allowed herself to hope that the long days and evenings developing a disruptive new technology product might finally start to pay off and that the financial pressures and strains they placed on themselves might dissipate soon. She thought how the prize fund of €100,000 might help them to finally secure the investment they so badly needed to launch the Mcor Matrix. For unless they secured a major investment soon, days such as these would be short-lived.

Mcor Technologies invented a rapid prototyping machine that enables a designer to produce a 3-dimensional model of their design at a fraction of the cost of a full-scale operational model. This enables the designer to evaluate the model, check the form and fit of the new design and get peer or client feedback, before a final design is selected. Rapid prototyping has been used as a design technique for many years – for example, sculptors would often produce smaller models of their subjects to evaluate from all angles before setting out to produce the final statue or work of art.

With the evolution of modern-day computer-aided design (CAD) software packages, the need to physically evaluate certain aspects of a product has been diminished by the virtual modelling and testing built into the software. However, models are still required during the later stages of product design when changes can become very expensive to implement. As the models are usually discarded after the design is finalised, product designers desire prototyping machines that can produce models quickly, accurately and as cheaply as possible.

Mcor Technologies machine is considered to be a 3D printer, which creates 3D models from CAD drawings by layering and connecting successive cross-sections of material. This additive approach provides a faster and less costly alternative to traditional machining methods, such as milling, where material is cut away in a subtractive process.

Mcor's 'Matrix' is the only 3D printer in the world to use ordinary/used A4 paper, making it up to 50 times less expensive than competitors' current technologies and the system is considered the 'greenest' 3D printer in the world.

The Matrix will initially target the following markets: education, dental/medical, architectural/design, gaming. Colleges and secondary schools will buy it for design classes. Dental labs will use it for dental records. Doctors will print models from CT scans to help plan complex surgery. Architects and design houses will print models of their designs and surveyors will use it to build topological maps to help plan reconstruction. Gaming enthusiasts will be able to print their 'avatars'.

COMPANY BACKGROUND

The idea for the Mcor Matrix first manifested itself in 2002 when Dr Conor MacCormack was working for a research company in Trinity College Dublin and saw rapid prototyping technology at work first-hand. Conor and his brother Fintan identified an opportunity to make a faster prototyping machine using cheaper feedstock. Conor, now chief executive of Mcor, holds a PhD in finite element analysis and a primary degree in mechanical engineering. He was student of the year in 1989 when he was studying in the Regional Technical College in Dundalk, now Dundalk Institute of Technology. Although still residing in the US, Fintan commenced work with Conor on designing the first iterations of the Matrix. These first forays were carried out long distance and their project meetings were held by phone late into the evenings. Fintan is now Mcor's chief technical officer, holds a degree in electrical engineering and is a qualified aircraft mechanic, having served with the Irish Air Corps.

Developing the product kept the MacCormacks busy for the first couple of years, until they felt they had enough work done to conduct a feasibility study with their initial target market (interviews were conducted in Ireland, the UK and the US) and a limited company was formed in 2004. The feasibility study was partially funded by Enterprise Ireland and yielded a sufficiently positive outcome that both Conor and Fintan left their jobs in June 2005 to work full-time developing the Matrix. They had funded all development work themselves to this point and would continue to do so to June 2009, through a mix of personal loans and by Conor remortgaging the family home.

Conor's wife, Deirdre, also joined the fledgling Mcor Technologies in June 2005 in the full-time role of chief marketing officer (CMO), in a real case of all hands to the pump in an effort to make the business work. Deirdre holds a Masters in Advertising from Dublin Institute of Technology and a BA in Marketing from Portobello Business College. She worked in Dublin and New York as an advertising account executive for companies such as Panavision and Golden Books in New York and for clients such as Cadbury Ireland, Carlsberg and Eircell in Ireland. Married to Conor, they have two daughters aged 8 and 5.

Risking their family's inheritance keeps Conor and Deirdre very focused in making Mcor a success and achieving their vision of having a 3D Printer on every desktop within the next 5 to 10 years. Mcor filed its first patents in November 2007 in Great Britain, followed by worldwide patents in November 2008. It has produced a roadmap of 18 patentable products to maintain a competitive advantage going forward to support its vision.

Figure 4.1: The Mcor Matrix

Rapid prototyping (RP) is the automatic construction of physical objects using additive manufacturing technology – that is, building up a model by adding layers on top of one another. A large number of competing technologies are available in the marketplace. As all are additive technologies, their main differences are found in the way layers are built to create parts. The Matrix uses a laminated object manufacturing technique (LOM) to produce 3D models using A4 paper. Competing approaches use plastic, wood, metal or ceramic as the base material for the model. 3D printer is the term given to entry level machines that are generally faster, more affordable and easier to use than other additive manufacturing technologies. The Matrix is considered a 3D printer.

Applications for RP machines include:

- Visual aids – enabling evaluation of building designs, parts or products.
- Presentation models.
- Aerodynamic analysis of designs.
- Patterns for metal castings.
- Patterns for moulds – for example, product protective packaging, etc.
- Physical representations of virtual images (game avatars, etc).

Figure 4.2: Examples of Matrix Output

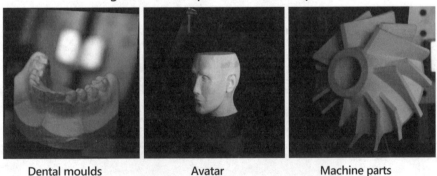

| Dental moulds | Avatar | Machine parts |

THE MARKET

Examining the market, it was found that 2,493 3D Printers were sold worldwide in 2006 (Wohlers Associates). Gartner predicted "the number of 3D printers in homes and businesses will grow 100-fold over 2006 levels by 2011, representing 300,000 units" (http://www.gartner.com/it/

page.jsp?id=593207) – at this growth rate, Mcor's Total Addressable Market is $7.5 billion. Gartner added "Printers priced less than $10,000 were announced for launch in 2008, which would open up the personal and hobbyist markets", although at the time of writing these are not yet available.

Mcor felt it could produce and sell its machine for $25,000 (€19,000), slightly more expensive than the average cost of the competitors' machines. However, as the Mcor Matrix uses paper to build the models, the cost of consumables is 50 times less expensive than the competitors.

Using her marketing skills, Deirdre is quick to point out that this means that a customer can get a return on their investment (ROI) within six weeks of purchasing a Matrix. Even if the competition were to give away their machines for free, Deirdre points out that it would still take less than a year (38.5 weeks) to recover the cost of a Matrix.

So who are potential customers for the Mcor Matrix? Initial research and brainstorming carried out by the MacCormacks determined the following target customers:

- Education.
- Architects.
- Product and other design companies.
- Online gaming.
- Medical clinics.
- Dental clinics (prototype dentures for fit).

and identified the following possible revenue streams:

- Machine sales.
- Maintenance contracts.
- Consumable sales.
- Bureau service (producing models for clients who produce models infrequently).
- An avatar manufacturing service.

Eighteen months after going full-time in December 2006, Mcor made its first sale to Trinity College Dublin, followed by Dublin Institute of Technology (Bolton Street) in April 2007. These sales enabled Mcor to put the Matrix through its paces and to have a client place different types of stresses and produce different models than those produced in-house in Mcor's headquarters in Ardee, Co. Louth.

While Mcor was starting to gain some traction in the marketplace, it faced stagnation in its relationship with Enterprise Ireland (the State agency responsible for supporting indigenous enterprise in the manufacturing or internationally traded services sectors), following its feasibility study. This resulted in the company having to fund the production of both machines themselves. In order to survive and grow their business, the MacCormacks urgently needed to build their network of advisors and influencers to overcome these immediate issues. Mcor turned for help to the very sector it identified as its lead customer, the third level sector, and Deirdre joined the Novation Enterprise Platform Programme (see **Figure 4.3**) in Sept 2007. This programme, funded by the HEA, would provide a range of supports to Mcor and would introduce the company to one of its most trusted advisors, Greg Byrne of The 3 Little Pigs Co. Although not recognised then, this programme also enabled Mcor to be identified as a High Potential Start-Up (HPSU) by Enterprise Ireland.

Figure 4.3: The Novation Enterprise Platform Programme

Dundalk Institute of Technology's Novation Enterprise Platform Programme (NEPP) is a programme of support for graduate entrepreneurs with an innovative business idea in the knowledge-based, high tech or IT sectors.

The main objective of the programme is to develop the commercial and job creation potential of the participant businesses. The programme delivers comprehensive training in business and management to equip participants to successfully start up and manage a new business. The programme assists participants in the achievement of personal and business development goals in relation to the project. It also assists participants in the completion of market or technical feasibility studies and/or the preparation of a business plan.

Since its conception in 2001, over 100 entrepreneurs have participated on the Programme. In 2008, NEPP participant businesses had annual sales of €27 million and had raised over €39 million in venture capital funding.

Previous participants include:

- Colm Piercey, Digiweb (www.digiweb.ie).
- Sean Gallagher, Smarthomes (www.smarthomes.ie).
- Peter Smyth, Redmere Technology (www.redmeretechnology.com).
- Michael Armstrong, Armac Systems (www.armacsystems.com).
- Jane Kelly, Big Mountain Productions (www.bigmountainproductions.com).

Asked what impact being part of a structured support programme such as the Novation Enterprise Platform had on Mcor Technologies, Deirdre noted that "participation on the NEPP Programme was a true milestone in terms of moving Mcor into commercialisation. It provided the company with a comprehensive range of supports and an ideal platform for networking".

EXPANDING THE TEAM

Before joining the Novation EPP, Fintan, Conor and Deirdre considered the company's strengths and weaknesses in order to identify what skills and advisors they needed to engage.

Three-quarters of the company's employees were from an engineering background but their skills covered a wide range of disciplines. It also had expertise in product marketing, advertising and PR. Deirdre's brother runs an accountancy practice, allowing them ready access to financial expertise. The company could also avail of the web design skills of another of the MacCormack brothers. Deirdre and Conor's parents also helped out by looking after the children and, in particular, with school runs.

However, the founders had little experience of leading or being part of a start-up or raising finance. They relied too heavily on their own resources and their ability to leverage their own financial credit rating. They had to learn what support was available and what different organisations could or couldn't support them. An early mistake they discovered was investing their own money early in the venture, as this historical investment is not counted for 'matching' funding going forward. They discovered that most State organisations require between 30% and 50% of the funding requirement to be 'matched' from private sources (the founders or other private sector investors). Of course, it does take some investment to get off the ground; a real case of chicken and egg.

Areas they identified where they needed additional professional input were contract and company law, shareholders and sales agreements and intellectual property. They also needed advice on raising finance and preparing themselves for the investment process and making investment pitches.

While Mcor made fantastic progress under their own steam, being part of a structured enterprise support programme made them take time out to focus on and plan for the future. Fintan and Conor were both still working 14 to 16 hour days, six and seven days a week, improving and bedding down issues with the machine. The prospect of them setting time aside to plan, to structure the business and to acquire customers was going to be difficult, if not impossible.

Availability may have been part of the reason why Deirdre was identified to join the programme but, because Mcor had naturally formed a team of diverse skills and Deirdre's background was marketing and advertising, Deirdre was their best bet to strategically manage and market the next phase of Mcor Technologies.

RAISING CUSTOMER AWARENESS

"Get this – it prints 3D objects on regular paper!" Guy Kawasaki

Working with their Novation EPP-appointed mentor, Greg Byrne, Deirdre developed and implemented a comprehensive and targeted marketing awareness plan that resulted in Guy Kawasaki, a Silicon Valley venture capitalist and one of the original Apple employees responsible for marketing the Macintosh in 1984, blogging[2] about the Mcor Matrix without ever seeing one and long before the machine was officially launched.

The ensuing publicity campaign saw Mcor gain column inches in a number of Irish national and regional newspapers, industry publications and blogs worldwide and an appearance on RTÉ's *The Late Late Show*. Mcor also started to dip its toes in the investment pitching arena by pitching at a First Tuesday event in April 2008, highlighting once again that the greatest obstacle the company faces is the funds to grow and sustain the business.

In October 2008, Mcor officially launched the Matrix at an industry event in Coventry, in the UK. The careful pre-launch preparation resulted in:

- 2 million website hits and hundreds of sales enquiries in a 10-day period following the launch.
- Development of a global sales pipeline of 1,200 leads.
- Interest from high-profile organisations such as Boeing, IBM, Autodesk, Frog Design, Nintendo, Nickelodeon, Stanford University, Panasonic, Siemens, Nokia, Hasbro, John Deere and Hewlett-Packard.

When funding for their mentor ran out under the Novation EPP in 2008, Deirdre was signposted to the Líonra Business Mentoring for Winners Programme, which allowed the mentoring and strategy development to continue uninterrupted and without placing a further drain on resources.

---

[2] Guy Kawasaki's blog entry http://truemors.com/?p=20637 is no longer available at this link following Truemors acquisition by NowPublic in 2009 but see http://www.digitaltimes.ie/2010/11/silicon-valley-goes-into-the-west/.

BUILDING MCOR'S CREDIBILITY

While a deliberate plan was created and implemented to acquire customers, Mcor also worked hard to gain recognition from third parties: industry experts and organisations, banks, State agencies and enterprise support organisations and any individuals who could help influence or assist their quest for investment.

This effort resulted in merited awards from:

- Inter*Trade*Ireland Seedcorn Competition 2007 – Highly Commended.
- Institute of Engineers of Ireland: Best Innovator Company Award 2009 – Highly Commended.
- Louth County Enterprise Board – Best Innovator Company 2007 and 2008.
- Ulster Bank Business Achievers – Overall Winners 2008.
- Inter*Trade*Ireland Seedcorn Competition 2008 – Overall Winners Best Emerging International Category (€100,000 prize).
- World Technology Network Award (for corporate IT Hardware) runner up – 2009 (Overall winner was Amazon; Sony was a finalist and Motorola received a nomination for the award).
- Finalist in the Irish Times Innovation Awards, March 2010.

To put Mcor's runner-up achievement in the World Technology Network Award in perspective, consider the R&D capacity of some of its fellow nominees, which deal with billion dollar expenditure compared to Mcor's mere thousands of Euro (**Table 4.1**).

Table 4.1: Mcor's Competitors in the World Technology Network Awards

Corporation	Sales 2009 $	R&D Expenditure 2009 $	Worldwide Patents Held
Motorola	22.0bn	3.2bn	23,019
Sony	85.9bn	5.9bn	N/A
Amazon	24.5bn	1.2bn	N/A

Source: Published 2009 Annual Reports of Motorola, Sony and Amazon.

Most, if not all, of the competitions Mcor entered required the submission of the company's business plan for scrutiny by a panel of experts. While this can be an onerous task, especially for a small start-up, Mcor quickly recognised the benefit of the feedback and insights from these experts and, apart from the time involved in producing the plan, this feedback is essentially obtained for free.

A review of their business plan commissioned by the Novation EPP was carried out by Brian O'Kane, Oak Tree Press and author of *Starting a Business in Ireland*. It yielded the following comments:

> "Great business – don't think that the business plan does it justice. Product Roadmap: Looks excellent – critical to progress this, but not at the expense of sales, which is what appears to be happening from the plan (as I read it)."

> "Don't think that strategy has been fully worked out – there are THREE businesses here: (1) R&D, developing new types of printers and variants thereof; (2) Sales organisation, to maximize value of R&D for benefit of promoters/investors; (3) Consumer business, offering avatars and models accessibly and affordably, through bureau service. The ONLY one that Mcor alone can do is the first – other people arguably can do the other two, and do so better. Re-think!"

Third party analyses such as this highlighted issues that could be off-putting for a potential investor and Mcor certainly did not want investors to walk away before they had the opportunity to meet face-to-face and pitch formally.

Of course, getting feedback was one reason to enter competitions but, like everyone, the MacCormacks also wanted to win. And doing so provided the encouragement to continue trying to get the business off the ground. As Conor himself puts it, "Winning the Ulster Bank Business Achievers Award (2008) is an endorsement of our business and what we say we are going to do".

PRODUCT DEVELOPMENT ISSUES

As the Matrix underwent further development and refinement, a number of issues manifested themselves. Mcor had built a number of prototypes and stress-tested them but the product was still not close to being ready for volume manufacture. For a start, it was too expensive to produce in volume. Mcor was sourcing parts in small quantities from intermediaries like Radionics and some key parts, such as the servo motors, were also extremely expensive. Mcor also required some parts to be specially produced to their own designs. These parts were sourced from a small specialist manufacturing company in the UK. This was also an expensive process and resulted in cashflow implications for the company.

Mcor also had to be mindful of its intellectual property rights. Filing for patent protection is an expensive business, especially when the product is still undergoing development. Mcor needed to ensure that the legal description of its new technology (the novel or innovative step in patent parlance) was wide enough to capture future refinements yet be specific enough to ensure maximum protection. Also, once an initial patent is filed, the clock is ticking down to the time the final documents must be filed and substantial patent fees paid for protection in the selected regions. To make the company more attractive for investment, Mcor's product requires worldwide patent protection which is also the most expensive (see **Figure 4.4**).

Figure 4.4: Typical Costs of Patent Protection

Search Fees (Patent Only)	Free using Google Patent and European Patent Office (ep.espacenet.com) €200 + using patent agent time-dependent
Filing Fees (approx) excluding attorney fees (gives a priority date)	Ireland €165; UK £20; European €1,500; Worldwide €2,000
Attorney Fees	€2000 – €10,000
Final Fees (payable 30 months from Priority Date)	€30,000 – 50,000 typical

Income generated from the sales of the initial machines was not enough to cover the manufacturing costs, patent protection and company operating expenses, as can be observed in the company's balance sheet shown in **Figure 4.5**. A balance sheet shows a "snapshot" of a company's financial condition. A standard company balance sheet has three parts: assets, liabilities and ownership equity and shows the balance between how assets were financed: either by borrowing money (liability) or by using the owners' money (owners' equity).

Figure 4.5: Mcor's Balance Sheet

	2009	2008	2007	2006
	€	€	€	€
Fixed Assets				
Tangible Assets	16724	19424	22740	25248
Intangible Assets	143160	134425	75988	24189
Total Fixed Assets	**159884**	**153849**	**98728**	**49437**
Current Assets				
Stock and WIP	6000	29085	0	0
Cash	6766	967	32619	7052
Trade Debtors	0	0	977	1064
Total Current Assets	**12766**	**30052**	**33596**	**8116**
Current Liabilities				
Creditors (<1yr)	**-180694**	**-124528**	**-112104**	**-80461**
Net Current Assets	**-167928**	**-94476**	**-78508**	**-72345**
Total Assets less Current Liabilities	**-8044**	**59373**	**20220**	**-22908**
Long Term Liabilities				
Creditors (>1yr)	**-57308**	**-102645**	**0**	**-3148**
Net Assets	**-65352**	**-43272**	**20220**	**-26056**
Represented By				
Issued Share Capital	144060	144010	94010	100
General P&L (Reserves)	-209412	-187282	-73790	-26156
	-65352	**-43272**	**20220**	**-26056**

To help manage its cash resources, Mcor investigated outsourcing the manufacture of the Matrix to contract manufacturers in Ireland. Discussions with a leading international contract electronic manufacturer (CEM) progressed swiftly. The key benefit of outsourcing is that Mcor would not have to fund raw material or other costs associated with manufacture upfront and usually the CEM can negotiate better pricing from component suppliers.

Unfortunately for Mcor, the partnership stalled at the final hurdle when Mcor could not meet the CEM's liquidity requirements. As Conor points out, "This was a major setback for us. We had spent a long time researching possible outsource partners and, having settled on our preferred supplier, we set about educating them about our products and market. We had built up a good relationship with the Irish operation. To find out at the eleventh hour that their head office was unwilling to do business with us came out of the blue and was a severe blow".

IMMEDIATE CHALLENGES

While product development has gone very well, Mcor faces a number of immediate challenges that will impact on the long term sustainability of the business:

- Funding – the need to get an investor on board.
- Cost control – cost must be driven out of machines, especially as sales grow.
- R&D cost recovery – Mcor must recover its substantial development costs. Its USP of low cost of consumables (A4 paper) is a double-edged sword as customers can source these elsewhere, thus impacting on machine pricing.
- Technical issues - supporting and resolving customers' technical issues.
- Operational – preparing for ramp-up to mass production and finding new premises or an outsource partner.
- Sales – to identify a sales and distribution partner in Europe and the US.

As the plaudits continue to ring out in the Ramada, Deirdre looks around the large conference room filled with successful business owners of the past, present and future. She knows that today a very significant step has been made towards achieving her family's goals. The €100,000 prize fund is already allocated and will be leveraged to secure €400,000 in investor funds and matched by a further €350,000 from Enterprise Ireland under its High Potential Start-Up programme. Like all things the MacCormacks do, this plan has been meticulously drawn up and is ready to execute.

ACKNOWLEDGEMENTS

The author would like to thank Dr Conor MacCormack and Deirdre MacCormack of Mcor Technologies for making this case study possible, through generously sharing information about their company and giving their time. A special word of thanks to Dr Cecilia Hegarty for her assistance in bringing this case to fruition.

QUESTIONS

1. (a) Briefly outline each of the elements of a S.W.O.T. analysis.

    (b) Using the information provided in the case study, conduct a S.W.O.T. analysis on Mcor Technologies and its founders.

    (c) From your analysis of Mcor Technologies' management team, outline the skills and human resources needed if the organisation is to grow to fulfil its potential.

2. You have been engaged to conduct market research for Mcor Technologies.

    (a) Using a fishbone diagram or another tool of your choice, conduct a market segmentation exercise for Mcor Technologies.

    (b) Which segments would you consider to offer the most potential or opportunity for Mcor. Why?

    (c) Indicate the most appropriate distribution channels that Mcor should adopt to reach these segments.

3. Outsourcing manufacture of the Matrix to a third party is a strategy that Mcor would like to follow. It would allow Mcor to reduce the cost of raw materials and would also mean it could manage its cashflow differently.

    (a) Suggest alternative outsource partners for Mcor and how your suggestions might overcome credit rating issues.

    (b) If Mcor was unable to find an outsource partner, what options are available to the company to fund product manufacture?

    (c) Are there any other elements of Mcor's business that could be outsourced?

4. Patenting is an expensive business but can be essential in making an organisation attractive for investors.

(a) If Mcor was to initiate patent protection on all of the products in its roadmap today, what would be the schedule of fees payable over the next three years? Assume worldwide patents and average attorney fees.

(b) What, in your opinion, are the main activities Mcor should engage in before the final fees are due?

5

THE GALWAY HOOKER

Pauline Ridge

CASE SYNOPSIS

Galway Hooker, a microbrewery, was started by two cousins, Aidan Murphy and Ronan Brennan, in 2006. Both young entrepreneurs are trained and experienced in the brewing and hospitality industry. Galway Hooker is a premium pale ale produced at their brewery in Roscommon. Aidan and Ronan have been successful in gaining distribution nationwide, with the majority of venues located in Galway city. After a few difficult years during the start up phase, they are now in a profit-making situation and eager to implement the next stage of their entrepreneurial vision.

INTRODUCTION

"So, Aidan, our first Galway Beer festival done and dusted. Who knows, next year we could be in Boston at the big one [American Craft Brewers Festival 2010]", Ronan declared from behind the bar, while busily setting up for the weekend event.

Aidan admitted it was a possibility. The bottling of Galway Hooker was on track and their intention was to export the bottled product. Exporting seemed the logical step to grow the business. He knew it would change the operation from a two-man business to a more complicated structure. Working together came naturally to Aidan and Ronan; as cousins, they shared a passion for microbrewing. It wasn't surprising to their family and friends when they started Galway Hooker – a microbrewery in the West of Ireland.

During the festival, Aidan cast his mind back to where it all started: their road trip around the States in the 1990s. Little did they realise their tour of American microbreweries would sow the seed and inspire them one day to set up their own microbrewery back home in Ireland. Fast forward 10 years and, in 2006, with a Master's degree in brewing and experience in the hospitality industry, the cousins realised their dream. Galway Hooker[3] was born. Galway consumers selected the name for the beer as part of a consumer promotion run by the company. It is thought to be linked to a nostalgic revival of interest in the boat, Galway Hooker.

Now four years on, as Aidan and Ronan dismantled the bar after a successful festival, they found themselves once again discussing their next stage of growth, prompted by an enthusiastic beer drinker who remarked that, "This beer is so good you should be sending it to the Yanks, they would love it".

---

[3]   Galway Hooker also is the name of an 18th century boat, developed for fishermen on the West Coast of Ireland.

Business was growing steadily with good distribution across Ireland, but it was far from global distribution. In fact, volumes in existing outlets had not increased in the last 12 to 24 months. Aidan and Ronan knew they were fast approaching the plateau of growth in Ireland. They assessed their options for future growth: continue to expand into new venues or export to overseas markets with a bottled product.

Exporting would involve using distributors/agents, securing capital to finance the export operation and possibly working with a third party in a joint venture, all unfamiliar territory for them. Once again, Aidan and Ronan were facing a world of new opportunities and uncertainties. Would exporting be the logical next step for the Galway Hooker? How would they manage this new venture and maintain the existing domestic business?

BACKGROUND OF THE ENTREPRENEURS

The Galway Hooker microbrewery was started by entrepreneurs: Aidan Murphy and Ronan Brennan in 2006 as a partnership, with each cousin having a 50% share. Both Aidan and Ronan have a food and drinks background: Aidan, a native of Cork, studied brewery in the Herriot Watt University in Scotland and gained experience working in breweries in the UK. Ronan, from Galway, studied hotel management in GMIT and worked in the hospitality industry since leaving college in the 1990s. In addition to being cousins, Aidan and Ronan share a keen interest in the world of microbreweries. On a visit to the US, they were inspired by the microbrewery industry there and the idea to start their own microbrewery in Ireland began.
After years of working in the drinks and hospitality industry and gaining in-depth knowledge of the sector, Aidan and Ronan, both in their 30s, decided to exercise their entrepreneurial dream.

Like most entrepreneurs, Aidan and Ronan contemplated starting their own business for a period of time before the idea transformed into a business reality. After 10 years of work experience gained in the breweries in England and Ireland, they made the decision to start their own microbrewery and, within 12 months, they were in production. Evaluating the viability of the enterprise was conducted with the assistance of the Roscommon County Enterprise Board. The Board provided a feasibility grant of €6,000 that was used to research customers (pubs, hotels, and restaurants).

Their first decision was deciding which type of beer to produce. Aidan's research on microbreweries (conducted as part of his Master's degree) proved invaluable as a starting point. From there, they interviewed microbrewers and publicans with regard to market potential. Foreign markets (in particular, the US) were found to be an excellent source of ideas and information. Aidan and Ronan toured the best practice microbreweries in the US. Trade journals also were used to identify size and trends in the market and to gain an understanding of market dynamics. Research findings pointed to producing a lager product. However, both Aidan and Ronan believed the lager market was highly saturated with several competitors. With Diageo and Heineken (two main players in the market) deriving the bulk of their revenue from the lager segment, Galway Hooker would be targeted as a threat. Success is dependent on distribution and, knowing that Diageo and Heineken would have the strength to influence distribution, they were reluctant to enter a highly competitive market. Therefore, they choose to focus on adopting a differentiation strategy, which resulted in producing an ale beer. Moreover, an ale beer can be produced in a slightly shorter time period than lager. However, the difference in production costs between a lager and ale beer is negligible. "The fundamental difference between lager and ale relates to the different functions of the yeasts used to produce the two beers", according to Aidan.

Early on, at the beginning of the operation, the dream nearly ended before it began. The decision to outsource the brewing process resulted in the quality of the beer being compromised. Their first task as new entrepreneurs was finding a solution to this problem.

Aidan and Ronan moved swiftly to counteract the potential damage and decided to take control of the brewing process themselves by setting up their own microbrewing facility. Their immediate challenge was to find a location for their brewery. Luck played a role here when they discovered a disused brewery in Roscommon, a Canadian-built brewery that was established by local entrepreneurs. As a result of this good fortune, set-up costs for the operation were reduced and the company started with approximately €20,000 for equipment and raw materials.

Once production began, they started marketing and selling their beer: a beer that still required a name. Using PR wherever possible, they raised the profile of the company. After setting up their website, they launched a competition inviting the public to name the beer; this was supported in the local newspapers, namely the *Galway Advertiser*. Entries were shortlisted to five, and from there the winner was selected. The Galway Hooker was ready for its official launch.

Identifying customers was their next objective; the local PR raised their profile and this helped to gain access to local publicans and secure distribution. Using their network contacts and cold-calling, they received a positive response; they found publicans welcomed smaller brands into the market. In a short time, they had extended distribution beyond Galway and had Galway Hooker pouring in locations in Dublin, Cork, Limerick, Sligo, Leitrim, Roscommon and Donegal. Their initial financial performance projections matched actual results quite closely, reinforcing Aidan and Ronan's knowledge of the industry.

Now established, the next step for the brand is to continue growth by increasing distribution and producing Galway Hooker in a bottle format. Aidan and Ronan had planned on launching the Galway Hooker bottle in the Spring of 2011 but are still in the process of researching this idea. In the meantime, they have bought new tanks to facilitate bottling on-site.

COMPANY BACKGROUND

Galway Hooker is a handcrafted premium pale ale targeted at a niche market that focuses on the discerning drinker who has graduated from other beers. Currently in a period of growth, the brand has managed to achieve a strong following among drinkers and the trade. Moreover, Galway Hooker has won the Bridgestone Quality award in 2007 a year after its launch. The influential *Lonely Planet Guide* recommends that drinking Galway Hooker is a definite experience that visitors should have during their stay in Ireland.

Hops and malt are the key ingredients of Galway Hooker and the aim is to ensure the right balance of both ingredients is extracted to produce the signature Galway Hooker ale. The company produces ale in 650-litre batches to maintain quality and exclusivity. Spending six weeks fermenting and conditioning is part of the process, as no chemicals are added.

Similar to other entrepreneurs at this stage in the business, Aidan and Ronan are directly involved in the day-to-day activities. Aidan is responsible for brewing and Ronan manages the deliveries. Large volume customers receive weekly deliveries, with the remaining customers receiving monthly deliveries. All customers receive a monthly service call – where the lines are cleaned, which is essential in maintaining a quality product.

After overcoming a difficult first year in business where no profit was made, Aidan and Ronan have now turned Galway Hooker into a profit-making operation. As a result, they are eager to maintain momentum and are planning for the next stage of the growth. Particular areas of growth have been restricted in the past, due to human resources limitations. Both Aidan and Ronan are operating at full capacity with producing and distributing the draught product. However, they recently hired another person in production and invested in more tanks, which will increase capacity and facilitate the bottling of Galway Hooker.

In addition, Aidan and Ronan will be working closely with the brewpub, Porterhouse, which will be responsible for bottling. The key advantage of having a bottle format is that there will be an opportunity to export. Irish microbreweries export 90% of their total volume, due to the domestic market being small (Corish and Hoey, 2005). Exporting spreads the risk and reduces the dependency on the Irish market. In order to be viable and cost-effective, large volumes are required. Aidan realises a substantial investment will be required. Until now, Aidan and Ronan have focused on growing the business at a sustainable rate. Their approach has enabled them to fund expansion using their own funds, unlike other businesses at this stage where lack of funds restrict growth. However, exporting will require additional resources, both financial and non financial, including a joint venture with a distributor with knowledge of export markets.

In addition, the bottle can be used to capitalise on the domestic off-trade market which continues to grow. Capturing the stay-at-home drinker will expand the market beyond the pub and restaurant. Moreover, it will spread the risk of dependency on one product.

However, Aidan also knew there was a risk that the bottled format may affect the image of the draught product if the quality cannot be replicated. Price will also be an issue, as consumers in off-licences are more price conscious than drinkers in pubs. Cannibalisation is also a risk, as drinkers may opt to swap their pint at the pub for a pint at home. If the bottled format is made available in pubs, the risk of cannibalisation is greater.

The case writer conducted some market research among draught drinkers of Galway Hooker and, on the whole, found that the bottled product was not favoured (see **Appendix A** for a list of venues). Publicans believe that drinkers (especially tourists) prefer the draught pint. The Bull & Castle in Dublin stated that the Porterhouse brewpub produces microbeer in bottles but only sells bottles in off-licences. However, when interviewed, the Porterhouse bar manager revealed that "ales in a bottle are a big seller". Clearly, further research is required if the bottle is to be sold in pubs.

The bottled product needs to address a new segment of the market (export or off-trade) not serviced by the draught product. Introducing the bottle will require careful management if launched in the Irish market, as the image of the draught product needs to be maintained.

Market Size

The beer landscape in Ireland has traditionally been dominated by Diageo and Heineken, representing approximately 99% of all beer sold in Ireland with microbreweries holding 1% (Carbery, 2005). Within this sector, lager dominates over ales as outlined in **Figure 5.1**.

Figure 5.1: Beer Market Overview 2008

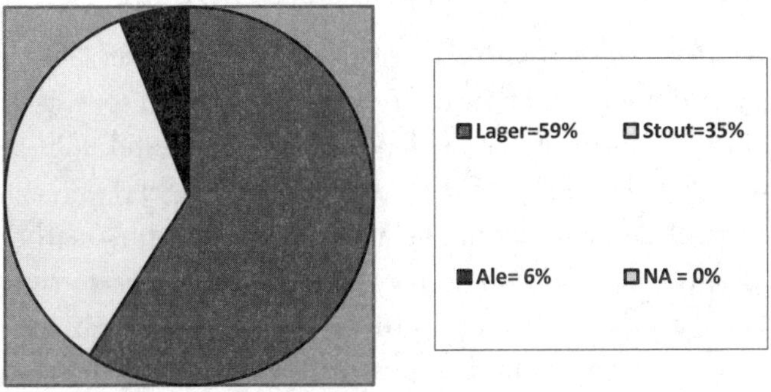

| ■ Lager=59% | □ Stout=35% |
| ■ Ale= 6% | □ NA = 0% |

Source: Irish Beer Market Report 2008 – IBA.

As a result of consolidation over the last 50 years, the number of microbreweries declined. During the 1980s, there was a brief revival of microbreweries prompted by the success of the US microbrewing industry. This was short-lived and the present industry did not materialise until the mid-1990s (Corish and Hoey, 2005). At present, there is no official data on microbreweries in Ireland, due to the market being quite small. In addition, the Brewers and Maltsters Guild of Ireland (1996), which represented the majority of microbreweries, has disbanded.

Financing the Venture

In addition to a feasibility grant, the Roscommon County Enterprise Board also provided a mentor, who helped Aidan and Ronan develop their business plan. Other sources of finance included a bank loan and employment grants from the Roscommon County Enterprise Board of €15,000. Both Aidan and Ronan contributed €15,000 each into the business, which was part-funded by their families.

Once the finance had been secured, their next challenge was to identify premises. Originally, they hoped to locate the brewery in Galway as they believed Galway was an ideal market, due to the large number of students and tourists living in and visiting the city. Unfortunately, they were unsuccessful, but managed to discover a disused brewery in Roscommon. The ex-brewery contained much of the required equipment, which reduced set-up costs to approximately €20,000.

KEY TRENDS IN THE MICROBREWERY INDUSTRY

Tourists are significant

Similar to other sectors in the hospitality industry, tourists play a significant role in the growth of Galway Hooker. For hotels and pubs located in tourist areas, the volume attributed to tourist customers was as high as 70%[4]. Interestingly, tourists did not fall into one demographic, with publicans stating that tourist drinkers were men and women across all age groups. In comparison, the local target market was predominately males 35+. Galway Hooker's counter mount was usually the first introduction to the brand and publicans believe that the premium quality of the counter-mount attracted attention. Moreover, the name – Galway Hooker – is the most distinguishing aspect of the beer. Tourists are keen to know the origins of Galway Hooker and how the beer got its name. The name is a real talking point and stimulates interest from tourists.

Association with food

Food association has been attempted by the major breweries in the past. However, microbreweries like Galway Hooker that do not use chemicals or preservatives would provide added credibility to any food association. Linking Galway Hooker with certain foods could add another dimension to the beer for tourists and locals, similar to the pairing of Guinness with oysters.

Changing taste buds

Many of the venues interviewed agreed that taste buds are changing in Ireland, but there is still a dominant level of lager drinkers in the market. Generally,

---

[4] Venue interviews, 2010.

the opinion from venues is that more needs to be done to educate drinkers on the unique taste of Galway Hooker. Suggestions include educating the bar staff on the taste of the ale, so they can sell Galway Hooker to potential drinkers. Other ideas include producing a small leaflet/postcard describing the beer and its origins.

Growth of European Microbeers

Whilst from one perspective, European microbeers are competitors to Galway Hooker, they play a role in introducing microbeer to the uninitiated drinker and this in turn grows the category. If these drinkers remain in the category, they will in time discover Galway Hooker as an Irish alternative to Belgian microbeer. Galway Hooker will benefit in the long term. As Aidan from Galway Hooker commented, "If we can grow the microbeer market in Ireland by 1%, all microbeers benefit".

Off-trade

The off-trade has seen tremendous growth in recent years at the expense of the on-trade due to low prices in off-licences. Lagers have benefited from this shift in volume; however, drinks normally consumed in a draught format have suffered greatly, namely stout and ale. Global brands like Guinness have seen a major decrease in sales and are working with venues to encourage drinkers back into pubs and bars (O'Dwyer, 2010). A summary of these key trends and the likely impact for Galway Hooker is outlined in **Table 5.1**. Focusing on one or two trends may benefit the brand in terms of growth.

Table 5.1: Effect of Trends on the Galway Hooker Draught Product

Trend	Effect on Galway Hooker if trend realised	Ease of capitalising on trend	Time before effect is realised
Tourists	Positive	Very good	Short/medium term
Food association	Positive	Very good	Short/medium term
Changing taste buds	Positive	Difficult	Long term
Growth of European Microbeers	Positive	Good	Medium to long term
Off-trade	Potential negative	N/A	Short/medium term

MAIN COMPETITORS

At present, there are six other microbreweries in Ireland and two of these are brewpubs, as shown in **Table 5.2**. The competitors have been ranked by the number of brands they produce as volume figures are not available (as the breweries are all private companies).

Table 5.2: Microbreweries in Ireland

Name *	Type	Location	Origin	Brands	Lager	Ale	Stout
The Porterhouse	Brewpub	Dublin	1996	9	3	3	3
Messrs. Maguire	Brewpub	Dublin	1998	2	0	0	2
Carlow Brewing Co	Micro	Carlow	1998	4	2	1	1
Franciscan Brewing Co	Micro	Cork	1998	5	2	2	1
Trouble Brewery	Micro	Kildare	2009	1	0	1	0
Dungarvan Brewing Co	Micro	Waterford	2010	3	0	2	1
Clanconnel Brewing Co	Micro	Down, NI	2008	1	0	1	0
Whitewater Brewing Co	Micro	Down, NI	1996	17	3	12	2
Hilden Brewing Co	Micro	Antrim, NI	1981	5	0	4	1

*   *Website addresses of micro-breweries listed in References.*

A large proportion of the volume produced by microbreweries tends to be exported. Exporting is seen as a necessity for two reasons: the market in Ireland is small and Irish drinkers are less inclined to test new beers. However, for Galway Hooker, the main competition is not necessarily other microbeers but mainstream beers. Smithwicks (in particular) and Guinness were noted as the nearest alternatives to Galway Hooker, the reason being similar taste. Smithwicks and Guinness drinkers are already accustomed to a bitter taste. Therefore, adding Galway Hooker to their drinking portfolio or exchanging Smithwicks/Guinness for Galway Hooker would not be a major change.

Compatible taste is extremely important, as the research indicated Irish drinkers are conservative and very brand loyal. As a result, any change has to be minimal in order to be accepted. These drinkers generally fall into the older age group (30+ years).

The average price of Galway Hooker was €4.27, whereas Smithwicks and Guinness are priced at less than €4.00. In relation to the retail price, 50% of the retail price goes to the retailer, 20% to the government in taxes and 30% to the rest of the supply chain. As a result, certain volumes need to be achieved to make stocking Galway Hooker profitable for both retailer and the company.

CHALLENGES AHEAD

The company is approaching its fourth year in business. Long-term growth requires planning and resources. Aidan and Ronan are aware of this need but find it challenging to allocate time to planning. Despite time constraints that limit planning, their initial financial projections closely match with actual financial results, a positive indicator that Aidan and Ronan know the industry quite well.

Growth is currently achieved by increasing the number of venues. In the short term, this plan is producing positive results; whether this can be sustained in the long term has yet to be ascertained. If Aidan and Ronan decide to launch the bottled product in 2011, this also will necessitate further resourcing, including expertise in exporting and distribution in overseas markets.

CONCLUSION

As an entrepreneurial venture, Galway Hooker has successfully positioned itself in a niche market competing with various competitors. Aidan and Ronan's next challenge is to decide how to grow the company. Naturally, this will depend on whether they want to manage the company to maintain a lifestyle or build the company for long-term growth. In terms of lifestyle, both Aidan and Ronan admitted that the first two years were the hardest as they had little or no income. Moreover, they sacrificed established careers in their chosen fields. However, they enjoy the benefits of being entrepreneurs: independence and a sense of control over their destiny. Although they realise they will need to work harder to expand and grow the business, they have no regrets in setting up Galway Hooker.

Choosing exporting as an option to grow the company will involve raising finance and possibly entering into a joint venture with a third party. A full evaluation of exporting will highlight resources required, risks and expected level of success.

Back at the festival, as Aidan and Ronan loaded the last of the equipment into the van, Aidan kept thinking about the customer's comment from earlier in the day: "the Yanks would love it". Was exporting the right option? Would Americans like Galway Hooker? Should the US be the first export market? Aidan knew one thing for certain; both he and Ronan had to do their homework before deciding what the future held for Galway Hooker.

REFERENCES

Brewers and Maltsters Guild of Ireland (1996). *Press Briefing on Revision of Irish Excise Law*, available at www.beb.ie/downloads/IrishMicroBreweryExcise Proposal.doc, accessed periodically.

Carbery, G. (2005). *Make mine a Dubbelbock*, available at http://genevievecarbery.com/print/16_beer.pdf, accessed 17 March 2010.

Corish, C. and Hoey, N. (2005). *Microbrewing in Ireland,* available at http://www.dcu.ie/~oshead/BE401/lectures/pres438240c35b1fb.pdf, accessed 17 March 2010.

http://clanconnelbrewing.com/products, accessed periodically.

http://www.beb.ie/index.cgi?pg=39, accessed periodically.

http://www.carlowbrewing.com/, accessed periodically.

http://www.dungarvanbrewingcompany.com/, accessed periodically.

http://www.franciscanwellbrewery.com/, accessed periodically.

http://www.hildenbrewery.co.uk/beer_caskrange.html (2010), accessed: periodically.

http://www.messrsmaguire.ie/, accessed periodically.

http://www.porterhousebrewco.com/beers.html, accessed periodically.

http://www.whitewaterbrewery.com/index.php/home/beers, accessed 25 March 2010.

Irish Brewers Association (2008). *Irish Beer Report*, available at http://www.abfi.ie/Sectors/ABFI/ABFI.nsf/vPages/Sector_Association_-Irish_Brewers_Association~industry-profile/$file/Irish%20Beer%20Market%202008.pdf, accessed periodically.

O'Dwyer, M. (2010). 'Guinness Rewards', Waterford: Waterford Institute of Technology.

Venue interviews (2010). 'Telephone Interviews conducted by the author with Galway Hooker venues', March 2010.

QUESTIONS

1. Aidan and Ronan share a deep interest in microbrewing and knowledge of the hospitality industry. Demonstrate how Aidan and Ronan used their previous experience in the brewing and hospitality industry to assist them in starting up Galway Hooker. What other skills and experience would have helped them at the start-up stage and at second-stage growth?

2. How do they compare to other well-known entrepreneurs?

3. The decision to produce an ale beer contradicted the research Aidan and Ronan conducted, which indicated that they should produce a lager. Do you believe they made the right decision? Use information in the case study to support your view.

4. Which consumer segment is the most important segment in terms of growth for Galway Hooker?

5. Assuming you are asked to prepare a report for the entrepreneurs, what growth strategy would you recommend for Galway Hooker and why? In particular you should outline in your report:

   • Anticipated timeframe.

   • Estimated financial and human resources required.

   • Potential impact on growth for the Galway Hooker in the long-term.

6. If the Galway Hooker was produced in a bottle, should Aidan and Ronan sell the bottled product in off-licences? What would be the advantages and disadvantages of selling a bottled product in this sector?

APPENDIX 1: GALWAY HOOKER LOCATIONS

Name of Venue	Location	Type of Venue
Bierhaus – Henry St	Galway	Pub
Roisín Dubh- Dominick St	Galway	Pub
Monroe's – Lr Dominick St	Galway	Pub
The Blue Note –William St W	Galway	Pub
Massimo– William St West	Galway	Pub
Tigh Neachtain – Cross St	Galway	Pub
Townhouse Bar – Quay St	Galway	Pub
Sheridan's on the Dock[1]	Galway	Pub
NUIG College Bar	Galway	Pub
The Cottage	Galway	Pub
Twelve	Galway	Hotel
Lohan's	Galway	Pub
Bar No. 8	Galway	Pub
The King's Head	Galway	Pub
The Huntsman Inn	Galway	Pub
The Salthouse	Galway	Pub
The Spanish Arch Hotel	Galway	Hotel
The Skeff Bar	Galway	Hotel
Tigh Coili	Galway	Pub
The Malthouse Restaurant	Galway	Restaurant
Connemara Gateway Hotel	Galway	Hotel
The Western Hotel	Galway	Hotel
The Oslo Bar	Galway	Pub
The Bull & Castle	Dublin	Pub
The Porterhouse, Temple Bar	Dublin	Pub
The Porterhouse, Nassau St	Dublin	Pub
Anseo	Dublin	Pub
Ryan's of Parkgate St	Dublin	Pub
The Palace	Dublin	Pub
O'Neill's	Dublin	Pub
Lucan County Bar	Dublin	Pub
Cassidy's Bar	Dublin	Pub

Name of Venue	Location	Type of Venue
Pygmalion Bar	Dublin	Pub
Sin É[2]	Dublin	Pub
The Dice Bar[2]	Dublin	Pub
The Bierhaus	Cork	Pub
Tobergal Lane Café	Sligo	Restaurant
Scholars - University of Limerick	Limerick	Pub
The Oarsman	Leitrim	Pub
Gleeson's Townhouse	Roscommon	Restaurant
The Olde Castle Bar	Donegal	Pub

Key: 1 = Closed. 2 = New.

6

AMRAY MEDICAL

Sean MacEntee and John Sisk

CASE SYNOPSIS

This case raises many of the issues that arise in a typical small indigenous Irish SME. With 25 years of experience, Helen Johnston and her family are keen to make the most appropriate business decision that will support continued development of the company into the future. Amray has established itself as a reputable niche player in the medical supplies market and now wants to explore other associated avenues. In creating the company in 1985, Helen made use of her knowledge and interest in the world of radiography. Now, her son, William, who is an engineer is doing likewise by using his knowledge and expertise in an effort to generate business in the X-ray room market.

INTRODUCTION

As William and his mother, Helen Johnston, drove towards Lyons Airport, having successfully concluded the acquisition of KX-Ray Medical, their long established distributor in France, they chatted about the significant progress that Amray had made since William joined the company almost five years ago in 2005. They reflected on the ups and downs of running a small business and, in particular, the challenges of successfully developing new products for the healthcare industry.

Amray, based in Drogheda, Ireland, had been established by Helen in 1985 to manufacture and sell a new range of patented X-ray protection aprons for use by radiographers (an X-ray apron is a lead-lined garment worn for safety reasons by radiographers in hospitals). Helen, herself a qualified radiographer, had come up with the idea while visiting a medical centre in the USA in 1984. Over the following 20 years, she had established Amray as a reputable niche player in the medical supplies industry. Amray broadened its products range through the addition of complimentary products such as protective eye-wear. Helen was particularly proud of her commercial success in France and the Middle East. Helen was a regular attendee at the Medica Exhibition in Dusseldorf, Germany and Arab Health in Dubai, where new customer relationships were developed and old customer relationships were strengthened. By 2005, the year William joined Amray, sales had grown to €700,000 and profits were a healthy 40% gross and 20% nett.

A FAMILY AFFAIR

William always wanted to be a civil engineer. On graduating from university in 1996, he commenced his career with McNicholas Construction and followed this with periods of employment with TCL Ltd – another small construction engineering company. By the early 2000s, William was eager to set up home near Drogheda where he had grown up. His wife Maeve, a qualified dentist, was also keen to set up her own dental practice in Drogheda. The idea of getting involved in Amray first arose over a family Christmas dinner in 2004. Mindful of the need for succession planning and also aware of new market opportunities, Helen had suggested to William that his background in construction would be of great value to Amray if the company were to consider diversification into the provision of customised X-ray rooms in hospitals and clinics. Helen had become very aware of this particular opportunity as a result of her frequent visits to 'end users' in hospitals and her regular networking with consultant radiologists and oncologists. X-ray rooms are lead-lined internal buildings in which patients receive radiotherapy with the lead shielding outsiders from harmful X-rays.

EXPLORING NEW FRONTIERS

Following that fateful Christmas dinner in 2004, over the following two years William carried out research of the X-ray room market. He was satisfied that no major supplier already existed in Ireland and, more importantly, that export opportunities existed in Europe and the Middle East. Amray's existing distribution network was an ideal channel for the new product service. KX-Ray in France and Al Arab Trading in Dubai had proven to be excellent distributors for the company's existing product range and William was confident that they would do an excellent job in identifying suitable opportunities for the X-ray room products. He was aware that this diversification represented a major risk for Amray, as contracts of up to €500,000 were not unusual – something totally new to Amray. Also building market credibility for the company would be a major challenge for Amray. Essentially, Amray would become a twin product company, with Helen concentrating on the traditional products and William taking responsibility for the new X-ray room projects.

The period 2005 to 2009 had been a steep learning curve for Amray. Having spent time initially familiarising himself with the core products,

William had spent much time researching the market for X-ray rooms. He estimated the overall market size in Europe/Middle East to be approximately €500 million a year. He quickly discovered that market opportunities existed in both refurbishment projects as well as in new-builds. Contracts were generally secured through a tendering process. William realised that he required manufacturing capacity if this new venture was to be successful. Following a similar business model to that pursued by Helen years earlier, he identified a suitable woodworking/engineering fabrication operation and offered them attractive rental rates in one of Amray's units located in Drogheda. Here, they would carry on their own business, while offering Amray capacity/credibility for execution of new projects.

In 2006, Amray secured its first order for a small project located in Our Lady of Lourdes Hospital – a large multi-disciplinary hospital, located locally in Drogheda, Ireland. Valued at €100,000, the project entailed the installation of lead lining installation in a existing X-ray room. No profit was made on this initial project but much experience was gained from the assignment. Over the following three years, additional projects were carried out in other medical facilities in Ireland and one in Dubai. With each installation, greater experience was gained. In 2007, Amray secured its largest project to date in St James Hospital in Dublin. Valued at €800,000, it was a high-profile installation that could make or break Amray. Fortunately, it went to plan and a modest profit was achieved.

Seeing greater opportunities abroad, Amray decided to spend more time and effort developing markets in France and the Middle East. For many years, Helen had worked with a distributor , KX-Ray Medical near Lyons in France. By 2007, its President had decided to retire and Helen and William considered that the company could be an excellent vehicle for market development. Following detailed negotiations during 2008, a deal was struck in late 2009. William would drive the development of KX-Ray over the coming years. He realised that this was a major addition to his already-extensive workload – at a time when Helen was seriously considering retiring from the business. He was also conscious that he now had two young children and that his wife had a successful and growing dental practice in Drogheda. Work/life balance was always a key priority for William and he was keen to maintain such a balance in his personal life.

CHALLENGES AHEAD

During early 2008, Helen and William had participated in the Novation Business Growth Programme run by the Regional Development Centre at Dundalk Institute of Technology. The programme targeted growth-orientated companies eager to embrace innovation as a means of accelerating new product/process and/or business model innovation. Through this, Amray soon realised that its financial and management accounting systems needed updating. A new management accounting system was installed and the part-time services of an experienced accountant were secured. This meant that the financial integration of KX-Ray Medical would go smoothly from day one. While on the programme, William began to realise that other new complimentary products were required to fit into Amray's current price 'divergent' product offering.

As they journeyed home together in late October 2009, William and Helen reviewed the progress that Amray had made and realised that major challenges lay ahead if the company was to become a major player in its field. Ireland was experiencing a major recession and other countries were similarly affected. The 'chunky' nature of the X-ray rooms business was a concern (order values for rooms of €500,000 were not untypical, compared to an average order size of €2,500 for aprons). They both agreed it was essential to add a specialist-related lower-priced standard product to their product mix strategy. Amray now has built a solid product range of low-end standard products for the industry (see **Figure 6.1**).

William had been investigating the market for encapsulated doors for use in locations where hygiene was of paramount importance – for example, food preparation areas, swimming pools and so on. An encapsulated door is a laminated door, which is also seamless – without joints. It is typically laminated in Formica to a thickness of 0.8mm. William had experimented with using PVC as a laminate with a thickness of 2mm. This would be totally 'bug'-proof, making it ideal for use in hospitals (as well as accepting lead lining for X-ray rooms). He was very excited about these developments, which despite requiring capital investment in post-forming equipment costing €50,000, would provide Amray with another standard but more high-end product with generous margins (selling price €400-600 each).

Figure 6.1: Amray's Product Range

Room Shielding   Mobile Screens   Personal Radiation Protection and Accessories   Radiation Detecting Probe

Nuclear Medicine   Ionizing   Protective Eyewear   Viewers/ Illuminators

Dark Room   Non-Magnetic Products   Film Duplicator   Film Markers

Cassette Positioning

KX-Ray Medical (a separate company) in France employed three people in sales and administration and was on target to sell €200,000 for 2009 and a small profit was expected. In Amray in Ireland, a sales turnover of €1.6 million was expected for 2009 with a net profit of €300,000. Employment stood at 12 people: two each in management, in accounts/administration, customer service/internal sales, and design/technical, and one each in purchasing, despatch/stores, project planning and reception (see **Figure 6.2**).

Other concerns were Helen's desire to retire sooner rather than later, thus tasking William with full control of the day-to-day running of Amray. Amray had been run as a twin products company for over four years, with Helen looking after X-ray aprons and William looking after X-ray rooms. This could not continue indefinitely. William and Helen both agreed that many strategic decisions lay ahead.

Figure 6.2: Amray's Company Structure

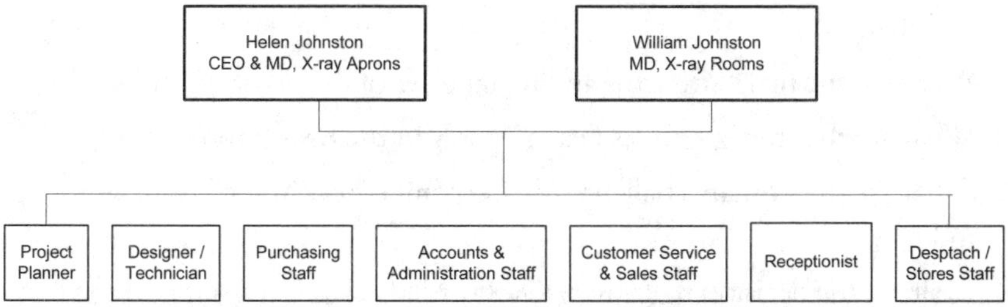

They both acknowledged the need for an agreed 'exit' plan for Helen, but had not given sufficient time to how they might go about agreeing and preparing such a plan. They were particularly mindful of the many personal relationships that Helen had built up over the previous 25 years and how these loyal customers might react to the news of Helen's departure from the day-to-day operation of Amray.

With a heavy workload, a new acquisition to operate, a diversified product range, a young family, a mother who felt it was time to play more golf, William realised that it was time to put together an integrated plan that would chart the future management and development of Amray over the next three to five years. He set himself the target of having the plan ready for January 2010 – which was only 10 weeks away. William's ambition was to have sales turnover of €3 million (made up of 25% Aprons; 50% X-Ray Rooms; 25% New Products) within three years and an overall nett profit margin of 15% (10% on X-ray Rooms; 20%+ on Aprons; 20% + on New Products) (see **Figure 6.3**).

Figure 6.3: William's Turnover targets

Aprons: 25%	New products: 25%
X-ray Rooms: 50%	

William knew that these were challenging targets but he was also aware that he had not joined Amray to have it remain a 'lifestyle' business.

QUESTIONS

1. Assess the market space that Amray operates in. Who are the main movers and shakers?

2. What are the main strengths and weaknesses of Amray at this time?

3. What are the strategic issues facing Amray in the near future?

4. What are the primary challenges facing competitors in the healthcare industry?

5. Evaluate the decision to acquire KX-Ray Medical. Do you support the move? Why/why not?

6. What are the key determinants of success in a family-based enterprise?

7. What advice would you give William as he begins the task of preparing his written plan for Amray?

7

ÍOMPAR LOGISTICS

Deirdre Bane

CASE SYNOPSIS

Íompar Logistics is a micro enterprise. It is located in the LINC (Learning and Innovation Centre) campus-based business incubator at the Institute of Technology Blanchardstown. The company has been in business since 2005 and provides transportation management services to a broad range of clients in Europe through their own operations and their relationship with BBA.

A new business opportunity, presented by BBA, has arisen, which will require the business to expand its operations into the new area of data entry. In addition, the company is beginning to engage in a more active sales and marketing campaign to broaden its customer-base for its existing suite of products and services. All of these decisions are leading Íompar Logistics into new territory and it is looking for guidance on the best options to manage this transition.

INTRODUCTION

Gerry Bedford sits at his desk at the end of a long office with his back to the window in the on-campus incubator at the Institute of Technology Blanchardstown. Like most founders, the solitary figure masks the complexity of running a small business in Ireland. Íompar Logistics was founded by Gerry Bedford, who is supported by Paul Coughlan, as Sales Director, and two administrative staff. Swivelling around in his chair, looking out into the car park, Gerry is pondering the next growth phase of Íompar Logistics and how the landscape of his office and business is about to change.

Íompar Logistics has been approached by their long-term business partner with a new business proposition. Gerry explains that this new 'chunk' of business involves data entry. He is hesitant. When he started the business in 2005, he "didn't want to get into that side of the business; the data entry space, I was adamant", he says, raising his voice to emphasise the point. Yet he was forced to consider that this proposal presents a huge opportunity for his growing enterprise and it would be a difficult decision to turn down.

Both Gerry and Paul have a lot to gain and to lose. Gerry is in his 50s, married with three children, while Paul is in his 30s and married with children also. Gerry started the business, having become frustrated with working for companies that were continuously closing down in Ireland. Paul, a former colleague, then joined him in the enterprise in 2007. With the Irish economy contracting in 2010, this opportunity presents a unique chance to expand in a difficult business environment. But Gerry is wary of the risks, particularly those risks associated with moving from a cashflow-positive business model to a more aggressive growth phase.

Gerry and Paul are reviewing the opportunity and are seeking guidance on the issues they need to consider.

COMPANY BACKGROUND

Íompar Logistics is a global provider of 'freight payment services and transport management solutions'. It provides solutions that identify cost savings through the efficient management of clients' transportation modes and process. Its primary business partner, BBA (Berman Blake Associates), is a US company that has been in business since 1972. BBA is the 'second largest privately-held freight payment service in the industry'. Together, the partners provide 'operational efficiency' and 'bottom line performance' through their logistics and payment management services. Íompar Logistics provides the critical European presence and 'local' knowledge for BBA, which is one of Íompar's largest clients.

Gerry breaks it all down by explaining that, for retailers and manufacturers, freight is a necessary activity. However, with freight comes 'every complexity known to man' as visibility of the freight process is murky when doing business in the global economy. Considerable savings can be achieved by outsourcing such services, thus proving a market for companies like BBA and Íompar Logistics.

Íompar Logistics is located within the LINC campus business incubator at the Institute of Technology Blanchardstown. Íompar Logistics has five customers, with the top two providing about 70% of its turnover, one of which is BBA. The business is cashflow-positive with revenue based on: (1) a transaction fee linked to the volume of transactions; (2) fees earned through cost reductions acquired by Íompar's expertise; and (3) an annual fee for account maintenance. Íompar sells 75% of its services to the international markets, mainly in the UK, Germany, France and the Netherlands. It provides a niche service that has appeal to a wide spectrum of industries. According to Gerry, "anyone moving freight is a potential customer".

Íompar has taken a bootstrapping (self-financing) approach to growth during its five years in business. Bootstrapping normally refers to the necessity (rather than a preference) for start-up companies to finance their enterprising endeavours based on owning limited resources. Entrepreneurs like Gerry must find creative ways of acquiring the use of resources without borrowing money or raising equity financing from traditional sources. They do not have to own these resources; but the entrepreneur has to be able to leverage them as necessary. Bootstrapping usually is orchestrated by a start-up absorbing resources from customers and suppliers in different ways, together with using resources provided by the owner/manager. Harrison and Mason (2004) in their Northern Ireland study, demonstrated that an overwhelming 95% of businesses used bootstrapping methods to a greater or lesser extent. These methods are summarised under two categories of product and business development in **Figure 7.1**.

Figure 7.1: Bootstrapping Techniques for Small Northern Ireland Software Companies

Product development	Business development
Special deals for access to hardware	Delay payments
Pre-paid licences, royalties or advances from customers	Barter arrangements
Development of products at night and at weekends	Personal credit cards and home equity/mortgage loans
Research grants	Discounted advance payments from customers
Customer-funded R&D	Below market or very low rent space
Commercialising university-based research	Deals with professional service providers at below competitive rates
Commercialising public domain software	Leasing *vs.* purchasing assets
Porting fees to transfer software from one platform to another	Purchasing used *vs.* new equipment
Free or subsidised access to hardware	Working out of home
Commercialising an existing shareware product	Gifts or interest-free loans from relatives
Turning a consulting project into a commercial product	Unpaid family member working as an assistant
Using public domain development tools	Loan Guarantee Scheme loan guarantees
	Severance and parachute payments
	Personal savings
	Reduced compensation
	Foregone or delayed compensation
	Special terms with customers, including discounted advances, prepayments and larger than normal deposits
	Outsource key parts of the business
	Shareware revenue stream

Source: Harrison et al. (2004), based on Freear et al. (1995a, b).

The relative importance of such bootstrapping techniques for product development is illustrated in **Table 7.1** below.

Table 7.1: Bootstrapping Techniques: Product Development in Small Northern Ireland Software Companies

Product development	Usage %	Deemed Critically Important %
Special deals for access to hardware	58	35
Development of products at night and at weekends	81	39
Research grants	42	19
Customer-funded R&D	58	19
Commercialising university-based research	23	8
Commercialising public domain software	39	19
Porting fees to transfer software from one platform to another	27	4
Free or subsidised access to hardware	42	15
Commercialising an existing shareware product	15	0
Turning a consulting project into a commercial product	65	35
Using public domain development tools	54	35

Source: Harrison et al. (2004), based on Freear et al. (1995a, b).

With the next phase of growth for Íompar Logistics presented by BBA, the company will need to expand its employee base from four to seven. Increasing employee numbers present additional opportunities – for instance, if Íompar Logistics recruited 10 employees, it would no longer remain in the micro-enterprise category but fit the SME category. Íompar Logistics is no different to 90% of the enterprises in most economies; however, the question remains whether this growth trajectory represents a rise in fortune for Íompar or a quagmire of conflicts. Gerry is faced with a profitable growth opportunity that requires serious funding. There are inherent difficulties surrounding capital availability in Ireland in 2010, as Forfás (2010), Ireland's national policy advisory body for enterprise and science, notes:

Firms cite access to, and cost of, finance as the most significant issue facing them today. This acts as a constraint as firms attempt not only to weather the recession and to survive, but also as they prepare for the upturn and invest in management development, productivity improvements and/or innovation as envisaged in this report. Despite some progress, there are indications of ongoing market failure in the availability of credit for certain categories of firms, especially SMEs – exacerbated by the current financial crisis. These are firms who can demonstrate commercial viability yet fail to obtain loans typically because of issues relating to risk management. (Forfás, 2010: xviii)

Small technology-based firms are perceived to be high risk, which imposes constraints on the ability of companies like Íompar to raise capital for growth. Winborg and Landstrom (2001) suggest that even those firms that face profitable growth opportunities may refrain from growth based on retained earnings or financial bootstrapping.

To provide some insight into the issues Gerry and Paul are addressing during this current expansion phase, Gerry explains the current service offering, the proposal by BBA and the growth decisions that need to be addressed.

GROWTH CONSIDERATIONS

Current Service Offering

First, Íompar Logistics provide freight audit and bill payment services as a third-party logistics service provider. Studies (for example, *Journal of Commerce*) have revealed that it costs more than $10 per freight bill to pay an invoice if paid through in-house resources. When this function is outsourced, cost comes down by one-10th or one-15th. The potential savings from outsourcing are reinforced by Aberdeen Group (2007), which believes that companies can save an average of 8.8% of their overall freight budget.

Íompar compares favourably with these metrics. For instance, take a pharmaceutical company that spends $100 million per year on freight distributed globally. Prior to hiring BBA/ Íompar, this company handled all invoices internally and there was no transparency or reporting capability around controlling freight. It hired BBA/ Íompar, which implemented a freight audit and payment solution. The company saved $7.9 million (€5.4 million), which is 8% of the invoices charged of $99 million (€68 million).[5] The savings were broken down in the following table (see **Table 7.2**).

---

[5] Currency conversion is based on 1 USD = 0.68479 EUR at 12 December 2007 per http://www.exchange-rates.org/Rate/USD/EUR/12-31-2007, accessed 10 December 2010.

Table 7.2: Fortune 500 Flow Technology 2007: Review of Freight, Audit and Payment

Saving Area	Amount Achieved $000m
Invoice Charged	99.3
Invoice Paid	91.4
Total Rate Savings	1.5
Total Duplicate Invoice Savings	6.4
Total Number Duplicate Invoices	29,582
Total Number of Shipments	1,425,649
Grand Total Savings ($m)	**7.9**
Total Savings (%)	**8.00**
Rate/Accessorials Errors (%)	**1.50**
Duplicates (%)	**6.40**

Gerry points out that Íompar Logistics has to remain competitive with the proliferation of competitors, such as CT Logistics, nVision, CTSI and Cass Information Systems, and Data2Logistics to name a few. If the company does not expand, it may be left behind. But Gerry is worried about the synergies of the existing suite of products and the new 'data entry' proposition from their primary business partner. For instance, Íompar Logistics currently provides two types of services: (1) an international transportation payment and audit service, and (2) transportation management solutions.

Firstly, the payment and audit service delivers the product/services shown in **Figure 7.3**. The service of scanning, data entry and document management is aimed at companies that only require the conversion of paperwork into an automated format, including intelligence reporting. Pre-audit and payment services require a more hands-on approach, as freight invoices are received, logged and each shipment is audited by Íompar Logistics based on a client's criteria to approve or reject payment. Gerry points out Íompar's market intelligence can cushion its clients from payment anomalies, which can present significant savings for their clients. A post-audit service involves a review of invoices already paid, where anomalies or overcharges can be uncovered on previously paid invoices "in the range of 2% to 5% of the total freight spend". Once such an overpayment is found by Íompar, it pursues repayment on behalf of the client.

Figure 7.2: Payment and Audit Services

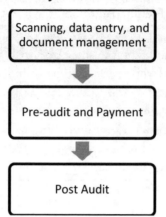

Secondly, the transportation management solutions component of the business presents a significant opportunity in itself. The global demand downturn has affected the volume of freight being moved around the world. Cost rationalisation has focused attention on better intelligence to manage spending on transportation and Íompar's clients are considering data analysis to be as valuable as the payment and audit services. For Gerry, Íompar's payment and audit process software is established for exactly that purpose. Gerry feels Íompar's current strength lies in its customer relationships, which are managed on a very personal one-to-one model. He does point out that this has the potential to become a "little more automated" in the future as the company gets bigger.

The Proposal

With the current suite of products, Íompar Logistics is making enough money to survive. But the company is looking to expand its customer base as more freight companies look to automate their freight management systems. In addition to the expansion of their current customer base, BBA, one of two companies that represent over 70% of the total sales of Íompar, has presented a business opportunity in the area of data entry.

In 2005 and 2008, Gerry considered entering the data entry market but thought "I'm not getting into that data entry game". However, in 2010, as one of Íompar Logistics' largest customers and business partner, BBA is looking for a data entry alternative to China, the 'data entry' market is becoming a real business opportunity. BBA is of the belief that there is insufficient clarity in communication, lack of knowledge of European languages and of the freight industry in both China and India. Instead of approaching these countries, BBA approached Íompar Logistics to provide these services. Íompar Logistics responded and were in a position to show BBA that, although doing business in Ireland is not as cost-competitive as China or India, Íompar Logistics held the knowledge, expertise and skills to execute BBA's data entry requirements. When BBA considered the deal, the cost/benefit lay with awarding the contract to Íompar Logistics. Gerry and Paul are now facing a compelling economic reason to expand Íompar Logistics into the data entry space. This comes at a time when they are looking to expand their current customer base for the existing product offering. Gerry believes both endeavours will be a challenge.

Growth Decisions

One of the immediate challenges Gerry and Íompar Logistics face is that of human resources. Gerry needs to hire four new employees, one of whom will hold a supervisory role, in order to fulfil the new data entry business. With data entry, a minimum number of transactions per hour are processed and, as such quality control is important, hence the need for a supervisor. In the past, when he has hired staff, he has used the services of the Irish National Training and Employment Authority (FÁS). By using FÁS services, some of the costs of a new hire are defrayed. However, he is cautious as his past experience informs him that, when placing a job posting at FÁS, you risk receiving a large number of CVs. In fact, a few years ago, he received 1,300 CVs in the space of 24 hours for one job posting, which was a very difficult process to manage for any micro-enterprise. Gerry is anxious to hire for these new positions but has limited time and the absence of additional personnel directly impacts his ability to solidify this new partnership arrangement with BBA.

Having made the decision to hire four new employees, Gerry looks around at his office and towards his two administrative staff members saying with trepidation, "Sure, the cabinets can be moved to fit more desks, they will fit in the current space". He knows it will be cramped and it is by no means a long-term solution. If he decides to expand the company, they will outgrow the current office space soon. Gerry does not "want it to get too big, too soon". He does not want "50 employees, maybe 20-50", with a "nice business and a nice profit".

When he entered the incubation unit at the Institute of Technology in Blanchardstown, he was attracted to the cheap premises, the possibility of having access to the expertise and personnel at the Institute of Technology and the LINC incubator, together with a ready-made labour pool from the student population. However, one of the most compelling reasons was the telecommunications infrastructure, which is vital for operating his existing business. The nature of his relationship with BBA requires large data files to be exchanged and therefore a reliable and efficient telecommunication infrastructure is critical to the survival of the business.

For Gerry, being located in the incubator has allowed him to grow in a measured manner. He has benefited from the M50 Enterprise Platform Programme, which is 'an innovative enterprise support programme, providing a range of supports over a 12-month period to anyone who wishes to start their own high potential knowledge-intensive businesses'. He started the business with his own funds. During his time at the incubator, he secured a grant from Enterprise Ireland helping with the commercialisation of research and development (CORD). Although not an immediate issue, Gerry realises that he will have to leave or 'graduate' from the incubator at some point in this growth trajectory. In the past, he has used the support network of the other incubates. Undoubtedly, he has benefited from the expertise of the incubation centre staff and it is to them he now will turn for advice on carving out a real estate strategy for Íompar Logistics. The LINC[6] provides an ideal environment for knowledge-intensive companies with growth and export potential and provides the following supports to companies like Íompar Logistics:

- Mentoring and advice on key aspects of business development.
- The academic expertise of the Institute of Technology Blanchardstown for research and development.
- Industry-specific seminars to support innovation and development for the companies.
- A cohort of students for projects, placements and graduates for recruitment.
- Boardrooms, meeting rooms, lecture theatre and labs in the LINC providing a corporate image for the company.
- The Institute's facilities.
- Networking events run in conjunction with other business groups in the locality to give incubation clients an opportunity to network with other business people to develop their concepts.

---

[6] http://www.itb.ie/IndustryInnovation/incubationsupport.html.

- Provision of group schemes for client companies.

THE MARKET

In addition to the new data entry business opportunity, Gerry and Paul had just started a business expansion programme to capture new customers for the existing service offerings. Paul, the sales director, is currently researching the market and Íompar intends to start presenting at trade shows where its competitors already have a presence. The company currently does not advertise for customers but is exploring the options that are available in order to infiltrate and saturate the market. The third party logistics provider space is becoming more competitive as technology advances and Íompar wants to leverage its European expertise into real sales growth.

The company has been self-sufficient up to this point. However, Gerry acknowledges funding resources may need to be brought in from external sources for the next growth phase. He has looked at sourcing these funds through financial institutions and State bodies but remains open to opportunities.

CONCLUSION

Having been in business for five years, Íompar Logistics is entering a new and exciting phase. Gerry leans back on his swivel chair and contemplates the changes coming. He acknowledges the role played by the incubator, not just as a real estate solution but as significant source of expertise and networks for Íompar Logistics. As Íompar Logistics grows, graduation from the incubation centre becomes a realistic possibility in the near future. Gerry knows the LINC staff will assist him in this transition phase.

The dual sales expansion programme will be demanding. On the one hand, Paul, the sales director, is working on expanding the current customer base for the existing product/services offerings. On the other hand, a primary customer has presented a new direction for Íompar into the area of data entry. The relationship with BBA is critical to Íompar Logistics, as BBA also provides the technological platform for the current product suite. However, Gerry is confident that the technological relationship is not of high dependency in that, if the relationship dissolved with BBA in the morning, Íompar could subscribe to a platform that would facilitate the same service.

It is Friday evening; Gerry has arranged a meeting with the incubation centre manager for next week. He sets out in an email the particular items he wishes to discuss:

- How to deal with the decisions facing Íompar Logistics?
- His desire to sustain historical growth.
- The constraints facing Íompar Logistics, such as:
  o Telecommunications.
  o International competition.
  o Poor demand in existing markets.
  o Lack of management time dedicated to developing new products and markets.
- The next growth phase of Íompar Logistics as it considers graduation from the incubation space.

As Gerry shuts down his computer for the evening, he knows he will have a lot to ponder over the holiday weekend, the big question is: How to manage this growth trajectory?

REFERENCES

Aberdeen Group (2007). *Winning Strategies for Transportation Procurement and Payment: How Leaders Are Taking Advantage of Market Conditions to Lower Freight Costs*, Boston: Aberdeen Group.

Forfás (2010). *Making it Happen: Growing Enterprise for Ireland*, Dublin: Forfás.

Freear, J., Sohl, J.E. and Wetzel, W.E., Jr. (1995a). 'Who bankrolls software entrepreneurs?', in Bygrave, W.D., Bird, B.J., Birley, S., Churchill, N.C., Hay, M., Keeley, R.H. and Wetzel, W.E., Jr. (eds), *Frontiers of Entrepreneurship Research 1995*, Wellesley, MA: Babson College, pp. 394–406.

Freear, J., Sohl, J.E. and Wetzel, W.E., Jr. (1995b). *Early-stage Software Ventures: What Is Working and What Is Not*, Centre for Venture Economies, University of New Hampshire, Durham, NH.

Harrison, R.T., Mason, C.M. and Girling, P. (2004). 'Financial bootstrapping and venture development in the software industry', *Entrepreneurship and Regional Development*, Vol.16, July, pp. 307–333.

Winborg, J. and H. Landstrom (2001). 'Financial bootstrapping in small businesses: Examining small business managers' resource acquisition behaviors', *Journal of Business Venturing*, Vol.16, No.3, pp. 235-254.

QUESTIONS

1. Should Íompar Logistics take up the offer of the new business? Justify your answer.

2. How, in your opinion, should Íompar Logistics approach its organic growth ambitions?

3. How, in your opinion, should Íompar Logistics manage the expansion of its existing customer relationships?

4. Explain the financial and non-financial risks attached to the organic growth programme and the expansion of its existing customer relationships?

5. What strategic human resource issues need to be considered by Íompar Logistics?

6. What working capital, investment appraisal and capital rationing considerations should be addressed by Íompar Logistics?

7. What are the financial and non-financial implications of leaving the campus-based incubator?

8

SL CONTROLS

Carol Moran and Cathy O'Kelly

CASE SYNOPSIS

This case study is designed to help students to explore entrepreneurial spirit and to delve into the entrepreneurial process set in the context of the engineering industry. The entrepreneurs in this case have achieved a lot in their first eight years of business and this case study attempts to highlight some of the challenges faced by small and medium enterprises (SMEs) from the start-up phase to growth and expansion into global markets.

INTRODUCTION

As they took their seats for the short plane journey back to Sligo airport, Shane and Keith contemplated what the future would hold for SL Controls. The marketplace in which they operated was as unforgiving as the crosswinds outside and they just hoped that the pilot was as focused and committed to a safe landing as they had been to the company they had founded in 2002. Recently, they had been asked to tender for a contract in the United States and had to determine what the best strategy for the company would be. Although SL Controls had previously completed projects abroad, it had never been asked to provide services on an on-going basis overseas before. Expansion on this scale would pose many challenges but, either way, they had to make a decision – and fast. The deadline for the tender was approaching and this opportunity would either lead them to a whole new level of success or potentially pose too great a challenge to overcome.

BACKGROUND

Keith Moran and Shane Loughlin first met at the Institute of Technology, Sligo, in 1998, where they had the roles of engineering student and lecturer, respectively.

When Keith had first gone to college, he studied accounting and computing. However, he soon realised that these subjects were not of great interest to him and were not areas in which he could see himself working. He therefore decided to accept a place at the Institute of Technology, Sligo, to study electronic engineering and this is where he first met Shane.

Shane's initial qualification was as an instrumentation technician. He was also a graduate of the Institute of Technology, Sligo and had continued his studies in Coventry in the UK. While Shane was working in the engineering industry, he completed his Research Master's degree and then had the opportunity to start lecturing at the Institute of Technology, Sligo.

As part of Keith's course, he was required to gain work experience in a relevant business and he secured a position in a local automation engineering firm. At this time, Shane had given up lecturing, preferring to return to industry, and also was working in the same company and so the entrepreneurs' paths crossed again. This was their first opportunity to work together in the industrial automation sector.

The automation engineering industry is concerned with developing machines, sensors and robotics that can undertake tasks that previously had to be completed by hand. This helps to improve efficiency, reliability and quality in the manufacturing process and other technological industries such as agriculture, environmental protection and building and medical engineering. Automation engineering is responsible for many of the machines that we rely on to manufacture everyday goods and other high-end products like pharmaceuticals and medical devices.

The company where Keith and Shane were working specialised in the area of systems integration. This aspect of automation engineering is concerned with introducing new machinery to the manufacturing process and ensuring that the new hardware and software of the machine can work with the existing machines on a production line. This was an expanding market globally and, as a result, Ireland was experiencing a significant amount of foreign direct investment. Many large multinational companies wanted to set up manufacturing facilities in Ireland to avail of the competitive low rate of corporation tax and gain access to a highly-skilled workforce. As a consequence, the automation industry was experiencing a growth spurt. Each firm with a manufacturing base in Ireland had to get its goods validated to meet rigorous high quality standards (required by health and safety legislation) and to ensure traceability procedures were in place. Keith and Shane could see the opportunities that this high level of investment was going to offer the automation engineering industry in Ireland. Having identified an opportunity in the marketplace and harbouring an ever-increasing desire to exploit the opportunities that presented themselves, the dynamic duo decided to go out on their own and start their own business. It was from here that the partnership evolved into SL Controls, the high-tech engineering company that they formed. They wanted to establish a company that could provide cost savings to manufacturing facilities through the use of world-class automation, integration and validation systems. Shane's reputation in industry as a top quality engineer combined with Keith's natural aptitude for business was a solid footing on which to launch the start-up. Keith recalls, "I had more of a business flair than Shane, I suppose, so I took on the setting up of the business, and Shane developed the technical side of the business".

ENTREPRENEURIAL TRAITS AND SKILLS

Before taking the plunge into SL Controls, Keith and Shane interrogated themselves constantly – they were concerned they did not have what it takes to be successful entrepreneurs. They questioned whether they would have the stamina required to withstand the hard work, long hours and commitment necessary to build a success. Any successful entrepreneur is going to face challenging times and they need to be sure that they are going to be able to sustain their interest and level of commitment if the company is going to be viable. How would they cope with the uncertainty and risk-taking that is part of the life of an entrepreneur? Did they have the appropriate skills set to set up and operate a business? "There were a few sleepless nights", Keith recalls. However, they could ponder their individual and team capability forever, it seemed; the only way to see if they had what it takes was to do it. But they did not jump in. Keith and Shane wanted to ensure that they minimised the risks by ensuring there was a market for the services of SL Controls and that they would be capable of meeting or exceeding client expectations. They considered the option of 'buying in' additional expertise if it was required, since they knew they were not experts in many different aspects of business. At the outset, they also broached the dreaded 'f' word: failure. Could they really cope with failure if things did not go according to plan? There were no guarantees; would they be able to secure employment if their venture did not work out?

THE BUSINESS PLAN

With a clear awareness of their own personal strengths and weaknesses, Keith and Shane combined forces to establish a vision for the type of organisation that they wished to create together. They would have to devise a legal and management structure for the company. They had to determine whether they would need to hire employees or whether they could 'go it alone' in the short-term.

As a first step, Keith thought they should establish clear objectives regarding what type of business they wanted to be in and then identify potential customers and how they could be reached. The range of products and services that they aspired to provide for their clients needed to be clearly outlined and then critically, the scale of finance required to make it all happen needed to be assessed. In order to do this, they would have to compile financial projections in relation to turnover for the formative years of the new business. Access to money was vital.

THE BUSINESS START-UP

The business partners had to raise capital to fund their new venture. They approached their local County Enterprise Board (CEB) and learned that funding was available for companies that were deemed to be a viable start-up. The funding was available for capital purchases, such as office furniture and computers, at the time of start-up, on the condition that it would be repaid after a three year period. In order to be considered for funding, a detailed business plan had to be prepared for potential investors.

Upon presentation of a detailed business plan outlining their vision, objectives, potential markets and financial projections for the company, they were able to secure some CEB funding. This funding, along with private investment, provided the financial platform for the venture.

In the short term, the company headquarters was established in a private house in Sligo, as the local business incubation centre did not have any available units and the local enterprise centre was still under construction. The first two employees of the business were secured on a contract basis, with an American multinational that had a manufacturing base in Ireland. SL Controls received its first purchase order in September 2002.

THE FIRST YEAR OF BUSINESS

Shane and Keith attended a networking event that led to another business opportunity in the Midwest of Ireland and this provided employment for two additional engineers. The workforce at SL Controls was continuing to expand.

The expansion of SL Controls' business, while very welcome, posed various challenges. A decision was taken to expand the management team, to ensure the required balance of skills needed to harness the potential of the organisation. In 2003, Darragh McMorrow became the third partner in the organisation and brought a combination of marketing and financial expertise to the equation; these key skills had been identified by the company founders as critical to the future success of the organisation.

The end of their first year in business was marked by their move into the recently completed Enterprise Centre, which provided office accommodation to businesses at affordable rates.

GROWTH

Global growth in the pharmaceutical industry led to the largest manufacturing start-up in Europe being based in west Dublin during the first years of SL Controls' existence. "It was the largest start-up at the time and there hasn't been one as big since", said Shane. This provided an opportunity for SL Controls to supply validation engineers to the site, on a contract basis. This site alone was able to provide full-time work for 10 additional SL Control employees. "This was the most significant milestone from a financial perspective", admitted Keith. This opportunity led to rapid growth of the organisation and presented new challenges, such as pricing of contracts and establishing terms and conditions for employees, in what was a very competitive market place with high demand for skilled workers. In order to maintain a competitive advantage, SL Controls had to ensure that they supplied top quality workers at the right price. "One of the main things we found with our pricing was we were a lot more competitive with our pricing than our competitors", stated Darragh, the financial director. Staff retention was a priority to secure continuity of contracts with their business partners. Financially, the contract with the big pharma company in West Dublin allowed SL Controls to sub-contract employees at an hourly rate, which was invoiced monthly and paid within 30 days by the client. This boosted the level of cashflow, which is the life-blood of any business.

SL Controls was awarded a contract to provide 24/7 automation support to a large manufacturing facility that had been established in Ireland. While this was a great opportunity for the company, it also posed some significant challenges in relation to the management of its human resources. Now it would have to incorporate shift work and provide suitable staff around the clock. The structure of the organisation had to be revised to incorporate the changes that inevitably accompany growth (see **Appendix 1**).

As the business continued to expand, SL Controls started to consider moving premises to a larger more suitable space. A site became available in a local IDA industrial estate, which was purchased by the company, at an attractive price, to construct a purpose built 6,000 square foot facility (see **Figure 8.1**).

Figure 8.1: SL Controls' New Premises

INNOVATION

Not only did SL Controls diversify in terms of the client base for which it provided engineering staff, it also developed software that helps to improve the efficiency of industrial machinery. Its Plug-and-Pivot™ software helps to improve overall equipment effectiveness (OEE) through optimising the analysis of the machinery. The software allows management to identify immediately where there is a blockage in the manufacturing process, thus reducing the amount of costly downtime, when equipment is not being used to its full potential. As Keith was keen to point out, "It will identify the area of a machine that has a bottleneck, so you get the most out of the machine by using this analytic software" (see **Appendix 2**).

Most recently, SL Controls have developed a process called DiVOM, which is an abbreviation for Design, Integration, Validation, Operation and Maintenance. DiVOM offers manufacturing facilities a complete process that can be followed right through from initial design phase to the maintenance of quality and efficient production. The DiVOM process has already been implemented on a number of sites and is currently being formalised into a process that can be packaged and taken to the market. Shane and Keith have had meetings with the Institute of Technology, Sligo, in an attempt to develop a course that would teach the DiVOM process to engineering students. This would provide graduates skilled in the process, who could be potential future employees for the organisation. SL Controls feels that the Institute of Technology, Sligo, is a good potential partner as it is a leader in online teaching of mechatronics globally. SL Controls is interested in sharing the learning from the DiVOM process, hoping to learn in turn from any feedback received. "You can be afraid or suspicious and do nothing or you can be the best at it and be known for being the best", says Shane.

Darragh, the financial director, and Keith are aware of the difficulty associated with marketing something that cannot be seen and touched. They know SL Controls should invest in marketing the DiVOM process so that they can ensure that it can be easily explained and sold to existing and future clients. This product is intended for export, so it is a possibility that the company could secure funding from Enterprise Ireland for exporting.

Customers of SL Controls who have used DiVOM on their Irish sites are interested in making it a corporate standard; however, they require that the process can be marketed at a corporate level to their counterparts in other countries. SL Controls plans to consult with the Food and Drug Administration (FDA) to ensure that DiVOM meets the pharmaceutical standards in the US. Since most of the pharmaceutical manufacturers are US-based companies seeking clients, it is important for SL Controls to understand the FDA rules, which are said to be difficult to understand for newcomers. Fortunately, SL Controls has experience already of working internationally, as it has completed projects in Russia, Slovakia, Switzerland, Germany, Singapore and the UK.

The innovation of DiVOM reflects SL Controls' ability to identify opportunities to develop new and improved services for its clients. By understanding the difficulties faced by its clients in the manufacturing environment, it actively seeks to invent solutions for its existing and potential clients.

BUSINESS CHALLENGES

The company had managed to diversify its customer base and secure new customers in existing markets. "We were getting an awful lot more enquiries from a broader range of companies ... there is a lot more potential work going forward", suggests Keith. Diversification was a key aspect of SL Controls survival as the company knew it could not become over-reliant on a small number of key clients. "At certain stages, we were only in one or two sites and there were threats of the contracts coming to an end, even though they would eventually get extended, but I suppose they were worrying times", indicated Darragh.

The expanding knowledge of the management team and company employees led to increased negotiating power. Improved networking skills, coupled with the company's growing reputation, provided valuable word of mouth advertising within the industry. "We have done a lot of good work in a few of the large multinationals, word is spreading about us and we are all making our own contacts", says Shane. The creativity and solution-driven focus of SL Controls has led to the development of successful industry-specific software innovations.

Despite the increasing opportunities, SL Controls is not immune to the effects of global changes. The external environment is changing and clients are now demanding fixed price contracts instead of invoicing monthly. Cashflow was an ever-increasing challenge. However, SL Controls not only had a credit crunch in the banking sector to contend with but also it had to deal with increased credit terms from many of its clients. Many clients who previously would pay their invoices within 30 days extended their credit terms to 45, or even 60, days in some cases.

This made it more difficult to secure a steady flow of cash into the business. In addition, many clients changed the structure of their requirements. Many companies moved from a monthly invoicing system to a project cost system, whereby the payment is made on completion of the project. Despite a healthy turnover, SL Controls found it difficult to secure additional credit from the banks and the accounts department had to work harder at chasing outstanding debts. Yet, even when things were extremely tight, SL Controls always ensured that staff were paid. It is the company's fundamental belief that, in order to ensure high staff morale, you have a responsibility to ensure that, even when the company is tight on cashflow, you must ensure your staff does not bear the burden through late payment of wages.

SL Controls had progressed from its humble beginnings to a 6,000 sq. ft. purpose-built headquarters, located in the gateway city of Sligo. The investment in this premises resulted in an additional opportunity for the organisation. With a lot of space at their disposal, the company directors needed to consider how they could use this to their advantage and perhaps generate further revenue for the enterprise. A recent survey had shown that "a substantial number of business firms are now stuck with surplus space that they cannot offload" (Fagan, 2010).

By the end of 2010, take-up of office rental space had increased by 40% on 2009, but this coincided with landlords offering reduced rents and incentives.

"Most companies moving into new offices have been very careful to book the precise volume of space they need and no more. The days of taking an option which provides extra office space are gone" (Fagan, 2010). Prime rents have dropped to the mid-€20s per sq. ft. – the lowest ever in 15 years. A recent high-profile example of how rents had plummeted with the change in the economic fortunes of the nation was a drop in rent from an original lease agreement of €37.00 to €15.00 per sq. ft. in order to retain the tenancy of the Electricity Supply Board in a prime city-centre office location in Dublin. SL Controls has plenty of space at its disposal. Some creative thinking is required to ensure that this was developed to its maximum potential for the organisation, in order to provide a suitable return on investment and to explore the possibility of generating additional revenue sources for the company.

CONCLUSION

Keith, Shane and Darragh have successfully carved out a niche in the automation industry and the challenge remains for them to continue to protect their market share. Continued innovation is the best way to ensure the success of SL Controls into the future. Innovation and finding solutions to real industry products is what the company is all about. "That's the main reason that SL Controls was set up in the first place really, to take the way Shane looks at machines out of his head and put it into something you can sell". The test for SL Controls will be to see if it is able to continue to expand the use of DiVOM nationwide or potentially globally.

Global expansion is the next obvious step. Despite the fact that SL Controls has already worked in the international market, it still has to undertake a detailed analysis of the international environment before committing to any new contracts. Recent research highlighted the lack of availability of skilled people and the ongoing problems of sourcing experienced engineers for some manufacturing industries. This forces companies to hire engineers with little or no experience and train them, which can take two to three years and leaves the company vulnerable to losing its investment if that member of staff moves on (Golden, 2010). Another important challenge is managing a team internationally. The directors need to determine whether they should employ Irish staff and relocate them, or if they should employ staff already living and working in the international markets they intend to enter. Given that their current international opportunity is for an extended period of time and potentially may require a permanent overseas presence, the directors need to determine whether they are prepared to take on long-term international projects. Completing one-off projects in foreign markets is a far way from having an ongoing international division of the organisation. SL Controls has the opportunity to undertake additional work in the US. The company has received enquiries for new projects. The entrepreneurs think that currently they do not have the human resources to commit to a new customer. They are afraid of compromising the company's reputation abroad by over-promising and under-delivering on product/service quality. Could SL Controls expand the business immediately or would it risk losing control and quality? The directors will have to make their decision promptly, as the closing date for submission of a full tender for one of the largest jobs is only three days away. As the plane comes into land, the directors gather their belongings and their thoughts, and look forward to finding out where the final destination of their entrepreneurial journey will be.

REFERENCES

Fagan, J. (2010). 'Office rentals go up as rents fall', *The Irish Times*, December 8.

Golden, C. (2010). 'Manufacturing Automation', *Technology Ireland*, November/December.

QUESTIONS

1. Should SL Controls submit a tender for the new opportunity in the US? Using PESTEL or another appropriate tool, analyse whether SL Controls should enter international markets on a more permanent basis. Assume you must submit your report to the company directors.

2. Assess the challenges presented by the expansion of SL Controls and provide recommendations in relation to human resource management to meet the demands of this growing company.

3. Assess the difficulties that SL Controls may face when trying to market a process, and how the company can overcome them.

4. Identify the future potential of the Plug-and Pivot™ software and the options available to the company in relation to this product.

5. Evaluate why SL Controls' experience in international markets may be of benefit when making the DiVOM process a corporate standard for its multinational clients.

6. Formulate strategies that SL Controls could use to ensure a steady cashflow for the business.

7. Provide recommendations to the directors of SL Controls in order to maximise the potential use of the 6,000 sq. ft. company headquarters.

APPENDIX 1: SL CONTROLS' ORGANISATION STRUCTURE

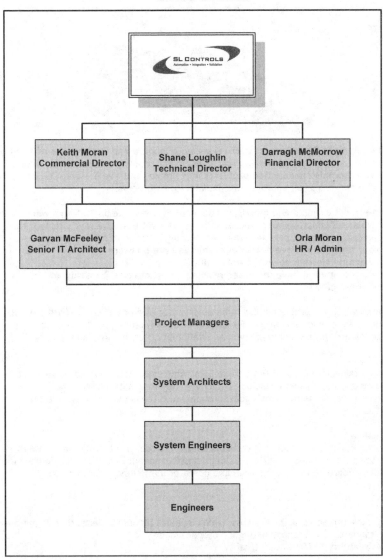

APPENDIX 2: OVERALL EQUIPMENT EFFECTIVENESS (OEE)

Overall Equipment Effectiveness (OEE) is a way to monitor and **improve the efficiency** of your manufacturing processes (i.e. machines, manufacturing cells, assembly lines). **OEE reduces complex production problems** into simple, intuitive presentation of information and helps you improve your manufacturing process.

Plug-and-Pivot is a simple and practical equipment performance analysis tool which helps you systematically improve your process with an easy, yet powerful user interface that allows the organisation of data for effective focusing of corrective efforts, e.g.:
- **Does your production have bottlenecks that you are unaware of?**
- **Is one machine slowing down the entire line?**
- **Does your equipment have increased productivity that could be easily and inexpensively tapped?**

Plug-and-Pivot allows problem areas to be quickly identified to a Station/Part level. It takes the most common and important sources of manufacturing productivity loss and places them into three primary categories: Availability, Performance and Quality.

Availability
Availability takes into account Down Time Loss, which includes any events that stop planned production. Examples include equipment failures, material shortages, and changeover time. Plug-and-Pivot's goal is to maximise the amount of available time used for production.

Performance
Performance takes into account Speed Loss, which includes any factors that cause the process to operate at less than the maximum possible speed. Examples include machine wear, substandard materials, misfeeds and operator inefficiency (performance efficiency).

Quality
Quality takes into account Quality Loss, which includes produced pieces that do not meet quality standards (the proportion of good product made).
OEE = Availability * Efficiency * Quality

This is an overall measure of the effectiveness of your machinery. Using Plug and Pivot, these categories can be acquired and refined to provide an excellent way of assessing where you are and how you can improve.

In any operation the hidden potential for improvement is greater than you may think.

CASE STUDIES IN SOCIAL ENTREPRENEURSHIP

9

INTRODUCTION

For too long, we have thought of entrepreneurship and enterprise as synonymous with the commercial world, with the ability to set up businesses and generate profits. However, this undervalues and under-represents the full potential of entrepreneurs and the enterprises they found. Entrepreneurship is not necessarily about generating profits, it is about identifying new opportunities and market gaps, developing innovative solutions, taking risks and delivering value. It is about being visionary, ambitious and persistent. It is about, as Ralph Waldo Emerson once said, not going where the path may lead but, instead, going where there is no path and leaving a trail.

Entrepreneurs are an essential component of any modern economy. The entrepreneurial mindset is an essential component of a healthy and vibrant society. Entrepreneurial ability to innovative, to launch and to develop high-growth organisations and to create value not only can be used to generate economic returns but also can be used to generate significant social and environmental returns. These 'social entrepreneurs' can provide a pipeline of new, high-impact ideas that tackle many of the entrenched social issues we face in Ireland today. And in doing so, they not only benefit communities throughout the island, they also contribute to the broader economy. In a 2006 Trinity College Dublin survey, it was estimated that the not-for-profit sector in Ireland accounted for 4% of GNP (€4.4 billion), employing over 40,000 full-time staff and working with over 1,400,000 volunteers.

It is within this context that we need to view the significance for Ireland of social entrepreneurship and social enterprise. As a highly entrepreneurial society, there is great potential to create a vibrant and dynamic social enterprise sector. However, the sector is still in its infancy. There is much that needs to be done to encourage and support the development of social entrepreneurs and social enterprise, particularly among the next generation of young people. The third-level sector is where some of our greatest potential lies, yet perversely it has been one of the weaker performers in terms of a pipeline of new social entrepreneurial talent – despite the capacity and genuine desire of many young people to contribute to society, to make a difference.

So why are we not seeing the third-level sector producing more new social entrepreneurs and what can we do to change it? The first action item is that we need to talk about social entrepreneurship and social enterprise more broadly across the sector. It should come as no surprise that young people are not considering a career as a social entrepreneur if they are not familiar with the concept. The second action item is to provide role models. We both learn from, and are inspired by, the examples of others who have gone before us. The third action item is to understand the process of setting up and growing a social enterprise.

In this regard, the social enterprise case studies contained in this book are to be warmly welcomed. They will make an important and significant contribution to the social enterprise sector in Ireland, providing the next generation of social entrepreneurs with powerful insights into both the benefits and the challenges of setting up and growing a social enterprise. In the two cases presented in this section, we not only see that many of the principles of entrepreneurship and enterprise are as applicable to community and social settings as they are to business but, critically, we also see the hugely positive impact social entrepreneurs and social enterprises can have on the communities they serve.

This casebook should be part of the curriculum for every third-level course. Entrepreneurship does not belong in the business schools of third-level institutions – if history, experience and social entrepreneurs have taught us anything, they have taught us that there are potential entrepreneurs in every walk of life. I hope that these case studies will help ignite that entrepreneurial spirit within all third-level learners, for it is in their hands that our future and our hope lies.

Seán Coughlan
Chief Executive
Social Entrepreneurs Ireland

10

COMMUNITY TOURISM HOLDINGS: MATURING OF A COMMUNITY ENTERPRISE

Seán O Coisdealbha and Patrick F. Scanlon

CASE SYNOPSIS

Many case studies are written about the challenges facing entrepreneurs and private companies. Very few case studies explore the dynamics, organisational development, strategy and marketing challenges faced by community enterprises. This case study explores those issues and traces the development of the organisation from conception (phase 1) in 1984 to phase 3 development in 2010. The case centres around how to successfully develop a community enterprise, especially the organisational structure and appointment of a manager. The case also looks at the Board's reactions to the 2006 findings of a consultant and their four main recommendations.

INTRODUCTION

This is what it had come to after years of struggling with this community enterprise. On a cold winter's afternoon in February 2010, it was the kind of day that had all the four seasons. It was 4pm in the Boardroom of Community Tourism. A meeting was about to start to decide on the roles and responsibilities of the new manager. The feeble sun had ventured out from behind the clouds and the rain had stopped. An omen perhaps, as the night drew in and the daylight disappeared in the West of Ireland.

Padraig, who was a voluntary board director since the beginning of the project, was already in the room. He spent much of his life around the tourism complex. He looked around, could see the golf course, one of the finest links courses[7] in Ireland. Other developments were impressive, such as the imposing clubhouse, the new administration and storage office block. He looked again at the course and saw the new nine holes taking shape.

The company had previously appointed two managers, one in 1995 who was funded by FÁS to develop tourism, but led to a split in the board. The other manager was appointed in 2008. He was appointed as a Secretary Manager (the traditional golf course management route). He lasted 6 months, as the combination of the recession (leading to a decrease in sales) and the increased expenses in running the golf course meant that the company could not afford him. The recent approval of a €150,000 grant aid package for a tourism development manager now provided the company with an opportunity to learn from the mistakes of the past and implement a professional structure to manage the company. The meeting was going to be

---

[7] A links course is the oldest type of golf course and comes from the Scottish word 'links', meaning coastal sand dunes.

very important, since it would define how the company would be managed over the next few years.

BACKGROUND: THE THREE PHASES OF DEVELOPMENT

The Beginning of a Community Enterprise

Padraig remembered the first few nights, back in 1984 after the local parish priest had called a public meeting to look for ideas to create employment. The parish priest in the 1980s was the local Catholic clergyman, well-respected by the community. He usually was in charge of a curate, or curates, and was appointed by the local Bishop and expected to be a spiritual and, in most cases, a community leader.

The 1980s recession was moving into its prime and the first meeting attracted over 500 people. They were the parents of emigrated children, the unemployed, the businessmen with falling revenues, and the lookers-on. The meeting attracted people from all walks of life. He remembered past meetings when he and his brother[8] and a few friends heard that around 1,000 acres of sandy banks was to be 'stripped' by the Land Commission. He had returned from England a few years earlier, an emigrant like all his brothers who worked on the building sites around London. He had made a few pounds and was now running a pub and a successful ballroom.

The first meeting agreed that a significant tourism project would be the best option. A second meeting was called. A keen member of the local golf club, Padraig and a few of his friends thought that a world class golf course on the sandy banks could be a major economic project for the area. They went to the second meeting and he and his brother were appointed onto the committee to develop a new tourism project. 100 people contributed £5 each that night. A few new golf courses had received significant funding from Fáilte Ireland. Could it be possible ... ? How could the money be gathered? What was needed: a golf course, a clubhouse? How much would it cost? How could they make it stand out, to make visitors travel to their remote area? Would the project be able to survive? Would the project happen without a community effort? The more they met, the more questions seemed to develop. But, a start had to be made ...

---

[8] Both had a share in the land.

The Development of a Community Enterprise

The next 10 years roll into one in the mind's eye. The lobbying for the State to buy the land, the formation of Community Tourism Ltd, a non-profit-taking company, selling membership of the company for £250. Luckily, the local community bought into the project and over 100 members joined the company. More initiatives were needed, such as significant fundraising. The legendry course designer, Eddie Hackett, God rest him, walked the land and promised to build a course that would one day be regarded as the best in Ireland. All he wanted was his expenses – for Eddie, this was to be the last course he designed and, in his opinion, the best. Three times the clubhouse had to be redesigned as the committee could not agree on the design. The licence agreement and fee negotiated by Community Tourism Ltd with the local golf club (the first of its kind in Ireland), joining West Coast Links to market the course, meetings with Fáilte Ireland, the County Council, Údarás na Gaeltachta, FÁS, politicians, etc. The weekends were spent working with a neighbour, who was employed at a major accountancy firm, to detail the business plans. He could go on and on. The grand opening in 1993 was the end of that phase. That night, when the golf club finally had opened, he thought the hard work was done … little did he know.

The Ongoing Management

Everybody told him this would be the hardest part. The same issues came up as in an ordinary business: sales, operations, marketing, human resource management, and financial management – the list was endless. He remembered how he ran his own business; he made the decision and that was it. But now, every decision had to be approved by the Board, which met on a monthly basis. The project was starved of capital, as no grant-aid was forthcoming for the operations of the project. The odd FÁS worker was made available, but how could the company promote the golf course and attract visitors? He remembered how the Board celebrated after the first week that generated IR£100 sales (six months after the course opened!).

There was no money to market the facility, no money to pay a manager, hardly enough money to keep the place open … There were problems on the course. The bar and clubhouse, well, that was a different story. The attempts to run the bar with volunteers did not work – for instance, some did not turn up at the right time! He thought about the attempts to franchise and the attempts to employ staff. He was deep in thought … going to meetings night after night to try to resolve the smallest of problems … How times have changed. Now the new structure was in place and a new manager was to be appointed to operate the venture.

Organisational Structure

Joe and Tom arrived together for the meeting. Joe, a retired schoolteacher, had been chairman of the company (Community Tourism Ltd.) from 1996 until 2007. He had overseen the development of the company in that period and used his negotiation skills and knowledge of organisational structures to guide the development of the company. The company was set up and run along a traditional community enterprise structure. As the company was unable to afford a manager, the structures for decision-making had evolved from the initial board when the company was set up to a fairly complex structure with various committees responsible for different aspects of the business.

This kept the company engaged with the community and gave people an opportunity to contribute to its development, but it was harder every year to get people to volunteer to serve on committees. The downside was a very slow decision-making process and the lack of strategic development due to people concentrating on ongoing management issues. The biggest difficulty with the organisational structure was the dependence by the company on the skill-sets of the voluntary committee and board members.

The inability to develop the business to a level where it could afford to buy in expertise (including management) was the core difficulty. Up to now, the company relied on Padraig's business experience, but a volunteer can only give so much. What would happen if Padraig was unable to commit as much voluntary time to the company? Joe had seen these issues and had engaged RBK Consultants in 2007 to conduct a strategic review of the company.

The review cost the company €15,000, of which 75% (€11,250) was received in grant support from a local development company. Although costly, the review was necessary because a Board of a Community Group tends to focus on operational rather than strategic issues, often due to lack of resources to appoint managers, and even when managers are appointed, the supporting system for the manager may be inappropriate.

The review highlighted that the current operational management structure of the company was flawed. The distinction in the role of the board in concentrating on strategic decisions and on governance issues was highlighted, whilst the need to overhaul the operational management structure by the appointment of a manager was the main recommendation. The formation of two new operational subcommittees to support the manager and to be focused on the key functions of the company (operation of the golf links complex and tourism development) was a second recommendation. This would encourage new people to join the company and could lead to new tourism products that the company could sell. To implement this, the review highlighted the need for a lean structure to manage operational matters and proposed that two members of the Links committee and the Tourism committee, as well as the Chairman of the company, would become an 'Executive Committee' to which the manager would be responsible and which could make immediate operational decisions as required by the manager.

A lot of discussion took place in early 2008 about the strategic review and, eventually, steps were taken by the Board in 2008/2009 to implement the strategic review.

The first step, the structural re-organisation of the company, was approved at the AGM in September 2008 (see Figures **10.1** and **10.2**). The bedding down of the new structure took place during 2009.

Figure 10.1: Community Tourism Holdings' Structure Pre-Strategic Review

A Tourism Development Committee was formed in late 2008 (after the AGM). They all had expertise, especially in tourism and were co-opted onto the committee, to join the four people appointed by the Board. They were asked to develop a tourism development plan. The plan was completed in June 2009 and funding applications made to fund the implementation of the plan. Before the completion of the tourism development plan, a manager was appointed by the Board of the Company in late 2008/2009.

Figure 10.2: Community Tourism Holdings' Structure Post-Strategic Review

The Power Struggle

The process of doing a strategic review highlighted two broad core objectives within the Board of the company:

- Developing and managing a golf course.
- Developing the company to enable it to be more sustainable in the general tourism market.

As the strategic review was being completed in 2007, these issues came to the fore. The two core arguments at Board level was that the company could develop best by increasing investment in the golf course and thereby increasing sales. The other argument was that the company could develop best by developing new products, whilst maintaining a high level golf course so as to have different income streams and not be reliant on one product. How the company could generate income from developing walking, cycling, nature and cultural tourism was reasonably vague at this stage.

As the funding application for a Tourism Development Manager was being developed in 2007/2008, it became obvious to the Board members that they preferred the golf course development strategy. But a Tourism Development Manager could be appointed if the funding application was successful. As they had enough votes on the Board, they developed a proposal that the company would employ a Secretary Manager. It was approved by the Board and the Secretary Manager was duly appointed.

However, the downturn in the economy, leading to a recession from mid-2008, resulted in a dramatic drop in revenue and, therefore, the Secretary Manager had to be let go. The approval for the funding for the Tourism Development Manager came through just after the manager was let go, but the conditions attached to it ensured that the tourism development strategy would have to be implemented by the company.

Joe, whilst not the current Chairman, spent a lot of 2008 using his skills to ensure that the Board did not split. The decision to set up two distinct sub-committees offered the best solution, as this would enable the people who passionately believed in each strategy to implement them. However, this methodology also had the potential to generate conflict for company resources, so the role of the finance committee and the executive committee increased in importance to facilitate a balanced approach to resolving any issues. How the manager would respond to the needs of the two distinct sub-committees would have a major bearing on the future of the company.

DIFFICULTIES – COMMUNITY ENTERPRISE

Managing Expectations

The recommendations of the strategic review were straightforward and looked easy to implement. From hard-earned experience, Joe and Tom knew that managing expectations within the Board and within the community was a core difficulty. Joe was worried about the appointment of a new manager and the expectations surrounding her appointment. Twice before a manager had been appointed; twice they had to let them go (one in 1995 and one lately in 2008). Would the third be any different? How would the manager relate to the existing committees and the seven members of staff, some who had worked for the company for over 15 years? Would the manager be able to manage these committees?

More importantly, would the company be able to implement the new strategy, as outlined in the consultants' report? The last time (1995) the company tried to do what the strategic review recommended (appoint a general manager), half the board resigned. At that time, those who resigned were adamant that the manager should develop tourism rather than operate the company and so they left the company to set up a 'real' tourism development company (now defunct). The recent experience when the company appointed a Secretary Manager, who concentrated on the operation of the course, was also a failure, as sales did not increase accordingly. Was the company strong enough now to develop new products in activity tourism as well as golf? Had the company any choice?

The usual chit-chat took place as they made the coffee and sat down to read the draft contract of employment. Micheal, Ivan and Sean would not make the meeting until 5pm. Padraig, Joe and Tom decided to start the meeting and try and get a few things on the contract out of the way.

Conflicting Objectives

The core issue of what the manager would be responsible for highlighted internal conflicts within the company. As a voluntary Board, people joined and served on the Board, but their reasons for doing so were often in conflict with other board members' objectives.

The title of the manager's job was the first item on the agenda. Should it be Commercial and Sales Manager? Tom found it hard to agree with this. He worked for the local milk distributor as a delivery man. A keen golfer, he had spent 10 years as the treasurer of the local golf club. He was one of a number of golfers who had joined the Board of Community Tourism over the last 10 years so as to ensure that the course would be maintained to a good standard and run like a proper golf facility.[9] The financial reality of operating a business like Golf Links (as the course owned by Community Tourism was now known) quickly poured cold water on any thoughts that members of local golf club had of getting enough members on the board of Community Tourism to control the business. Tom stayed on, interested in helping the company and his community; he was now the company secretary. Now, though, the company was about to appoint either a Commercial and Sales Manager or a General Manager, instead of the Secretary Manager appointed by most member-owned golf courses. Why not appoint a Secretary Manager, sure hadn't it been done the previous year (after a divisive Board meeting) and the

---

[9]   Only three of the original board members now remained.

course was in great shape? Would the Secretary Manager have worked if the right person had been appointed? It had been decided that the Secretary Manager should manage the daily operations of the golf course and also would be responsible for managing all staff in the clubhouse.

Lack of Capital

Prior to the strategic review, the company had concentrated on generating operating profits since the opening of the golf course. This had been a hard and long struggle, as the annual subscription from the Golf Club was around 25% of total income. The rest had to be sourced from tourists playing the course. Operating and management issues used to dominate the monthly Board meetings. At one stage, the clubhouse bar and restaurant was losing over €1,500 a week, the main reason being that a certain level of service had to be provided for visitors in relation to opening hours, even though the turnover did not justify this expenditure. Getting a franchisee in, even though it cost €40,000, reduced the management headache of the clubhouse facility. 2004 to 2008 were good years and the company turned a small profit.

However, in late 2006, the winds of change in the golf product in Ireland were beginning to blow. An increasing number of new courses opened from 2004 onwards. This was putting downward pressure on the number of tourists visiting the Golf Links and on the green fee revenue. The 2006 Ryder Cup spike was an exception to the rule; that year the green fees taken in September were over €100,000. The company was at a crossroads, turnover was around €500,000 but there was no manager and the company was run primarily by Padraig on a voluntary capacity. Competition for the sole revenue generator, golf, was increasing. The Board was getting old together – most of the Board had been around since 1994.

The figures didn't lie (see **Table 10.1**). Padraig, Tom and Joe knew that sales had to be increased and costs had to be controlled, especially in the current recession. The lack of consistent profit caused the company some serious cashflow struggles.

Table 10.1: Community Tourism Holdings' Company Performance, 2004 to 2008

Profit and Loss Account	Year				
	2004	2005	2006	2007	2008
Sales €000					
Course Sales (Green Fees)	210	235	270	355	302
Local Golf Club Membership	75	76	78	82	88
Shop Sales	40	42	50	65	62
Bar and Restaurant	90	92	94	0	0
Total	**415**	**445**	**492**	**502**	**452**
Operating Costs €000					
Course Costs (including staff)	130	135	150	185	177
Shop Costs (including staff)	35	38	42	54	55
Bar and Restaurant Costs (including staff)	150	145	152	0	0
Franchisee	0	0	0	40	40
Marketing	20	10	12	20	15
Manager	50	0	0	0	5
Overheads	90	120	125	160	151
Total	**475**	**448**	**481**	**459**	**443**
Operating Profit (Loss)	**(60)**	**(3)**	**11**	**43**	**9**

Availability of State Support

Community Tourism Holdings effectively reduced the pressure on voluntary effort via the appointment of a manager and bringing new people into the voluntary group with a new focus for development within the existing structure. By ensuring that the new structure accommodated both the Tourism Development Committee and Carne Golf Links Committee, both committees are able to work well together to enhance the product and service offering to customers.

The company had not received any State aid since 2002, because it was not considered to be a tourism development company but rather a golf course. The new Tourism Development Plan that was completed during the strategic review period was now beginning to source some external grant-aid and

Padraig, Tom and Joe knew that this would need to be well-managed and that the expectations of the funders needed to be met to ensure some ongoing support.

The Tourism Development Plan highlighted that walking, cycling, nature, marine tourism, event management and ground-handling services were growing areas in the sector that could be developed in the region. The plan was broad in its scope. It provided a SWOT analysis. It also looked at costs for the suggested investments and explored the commercial possibilities of a number of products. Since the tourism committee had begun working on the plan, they had researched and lobbied for key infrastructure.

At the launch of the plan in June 2009, the committee had lobbied hard to get investment in walking and cycling routes and Fáilte Ireland developed two walking routes (100% funded by Fáilte Ireland) in partnership with local communities. During 2009, a commitment from a number of State sources to invest €500,000 in cycling and nature facilities in the locality before the end of 2010 was given. €30,000 was also secured to provide a training course for guides. In the current economic climate, it was the view of the tourism committee that the focus in the next three years should be on developing packages to sell walking, nature and cycling holidays and to generate some income from running a few key events to attract tourists.

Micheal, Sean and Ivan were the prime movers in developing the tourism development plan. They had sourced €150,000 from a local development fund to support the employment of a manger to implement the plan. The commercial opportunity/role of the company in this strategy was not fully worked out, as the detailed market research had not been completed. The overall market trends highlighted potential opportunities; therefore, in their opinion, new product development was going to be a key role for the new manager.

Although Community Tourism Holdings required a general manager to manage both aspects of the group, perhaps the manager should have a key role as Commercial and Sales Manager. Initially, the manager could concentrate on golf products, as sales had dropped by 30% in 2009 and the company had an operating loss of around €40,000 for the year. In addition, the manager could do initial development work on new products in the three areas identified in the Tourism Development Plan, as well as developing training courses and doing market research for the new products. However, Community Tourism Holdings also desperately needed an updated website as a matter of priority, which would cost money.

In general, the meeting spent a lot of time trying to ensure that the responsibilities of the manager reflected the work issues of the golf course committee and the tourism development committee as fairly as possible.

Ensuring New Members for the Board

Ivan, Micheal, Louise and Sean were relatively new to the Board of the company but were in agreement on the role of the manager. The four of them were members of the new tourism development committee that had been set up over a year previously as a result of the strategic review. Micheal, a retired Air Corps pilot, operated his own water sports activity centre, set up in 1992, worth over €2 million and with an annual turnover in excess of €1 million. Sean (whose father was a successful businessman in the local town) had just opened a new Leisureplex centre with a total investment of €3 million. Louise was the marketing consultant for the relatively new hotel in town with 70 bedrooms and a 25-metre swimming pool. The hotel was trading successfully but wanted to develop new markets. Ivan, the principal of a local secondary school, ran a successful triathlon every summer. All four were locals and under the age of 40. They were now members of the tourism committee of Erris Tourism and keen to develop tourism, whilst ensuring that the company thrived.

They had spent a lot of 2009 trying to convince the long-established members of the Board that tourism development and the development of the golf course could be done together. In their eyes, it was just the company developing its product range to reflect changes in the marketplace and to increase sales by developing new markets and market segments. The dialogue during the year also highlighted the untapped potential in certain golf markets (especially in the UK) that the company had not developed, as its primary focus was on the home and US market. The bundling and cross-selling of product also offered some potential in certain market segments and in specific markets in Northern Germany and Scandinavia, where the average golfer was also an avid outdoors enthusiast.

IMPLEMENTING CHANGE

Short-term Objectives

The conversation evolved around the roles and responsibilities of the manager. The fact that the interview process had been successful this time in identifying a professional manager was a key issue. It had proved very difficult to attract a professional manager to the company in the past, as community enterprises are seldom attractive options for professional managers. Now the Board could work on the roles and responsibilities as broadly agreed in the job specification, confident in the knowledge that the proposed manager had good management skills.

After some lively discussion, it was agreed that the main reason for the failure of the previous two managers could be summarised in the fact that they had come from a pure golf course management background rather than a management background. The company had not developed a structure to engage with the manager. The expectations of the manager were not well-defined and internal communication systems between members of the committees and the manager were too informal. Often, the manager was getting direction from a number of different sources, both formally and informally. Upon further consideration, the following reporting sources of direction were identified:

- The chairman of the Board.
- Members of the Board.
- The chairman of the golf course committee.
- Members of the golf course committee.
- Members of the general purposes committee.
- Members of Belmullet Golf Club.

The new communication system agreed upon was that the chairman of the company should be able to have discussions with the manager at all times. All decisions and agreements on work programmes and reporting were to be communicated to the manager on a monthly basis by the executive committee. Tom wondered whether the head green-keeper should now report to the manager, who had no experience of managing a golf course, or to the golf course committee, whose voluntary members gave freely of their time and expertise in helping the green-keeper keep the course in good order. It was agreed that this was an important issue and was to be discussed at the next golf course committee meeting and that a recommendation was to be sought from them.

It was emphasised that the role of the golf course committee was crucial and that the efforts of the voluntary members was much appreciated. It would be difficult for a new manager to manage properly without having enough authority to manage key staff. The possibility of developing a quality system in association with the golf course committee was explored. It might be an option for the manager to help the committee and the staff to develop the system as a team, so that the golfers would be getting a better service. The quality of the course was not the issue, but more could be done about the services and especially linking or packaging them up to ensure that the golfers had a fulfilling experience.

Long-term Objectives

Micheal wondered how the manager could implement the Tourism Development Plan if she was to be focused on managing the golf course for the foreseeable future. A number of possible problems needed immediate attention. Targets, as set out by in the Tourism Development Plan and agreed with the funders, needed to be delivered. If not, the funding could be withdrawn. He mentioned that this might be a strategic long-term mistake for the company, since it had lost FÁS funding before for concentrating on the golf course and not engaging in developmental work. They did not want to fall into the trap again where, in effect, FÁS was subsidising a golf course. In fact, he was worried that, if the company did not develop its product range quickly, it would continue to suffer as the golf market had stagnated and that competition in it was fierce. Padraig agreed that this was a concern that needed to be addressed. He hoped that the executive committee could manage this over time, but that the survival of the company was also an issue.

Micheal said that his own company was very grateful for the new walks developed as a result of the lobbying done by Board of Community Tourism Ltd. with Fáilte Ireland and that his customers were getting great use from it. He thought that other tourism companies were also using the infrastructure, but that some kind of system should be developed to gather funding from the walkers (like the honesty boxes in the Monroes in Scotland), to help maintain the walks. Sean suggested that the company should seek to develop at least one element of the Tourism Development Plan and see whether it could contribute revenue to the company.

The three potential roles for the company in operating as a ground handling agent, an event management agent and general tourism development needed to be explored a bit further from a market gap viewpoint. Ivan suggested that the company might take over the organisation of the triathlon. Although he had only started it three years ago, it had 500 competitors in 2009 and there was going to be a championship race in 2010, which meant around 750 competitors. He said he found it very hard to organise it on a voluntary basis and that the triathlon made a profit of €8,000 in 2009 (granted there was no paid labour input). He thought that up to €50,000 profit could be made in 2011 if the championship race in 2010 was a success and if the numbers went up to 1,000 people in 2011.

After some discussion on this, the meeting agreed that the manager would present monthly reports to both the golf course committee and the tourism development committee and that the main work packages that the manager would undertake would be as follows for the first year:

- Review and make the financial control systems and structures for budgeting more efficient.
- Develop sales on the golf course as a matter of urgency.
- Concentrate on developing training programmes to develop the skills in the area for walking ventures etc. (for example, a guiding course).
- Do market research on new products and new markets that the company could engage with.

It was agreed that most of the thoughts on the long-term plans were very good and that innovative thinking like this was required. It was agreed that the Board would have a special meeting during the year to discuss these proposals fully and that the voluntary members should put some work into their ideas and make a presentation at the special Board meeting.

CHALLENGES FACING THE MANAGER

It was getting late. Key items such as marketing and sales, financial management, new product development and human resource management were identified as the major areas of responsibility for the manager. Whilst addressing these issues was not of immediate concern, a discussion took place on their importance. Padraig asked that the discussion be focused on marketing and sales, as it was getting late and the other areas presented medium-term issues that could be discussed in the future.

Marketing and Sales

Louise wanted to explore the potential to develop destination branding for the region. It would need the support and contributions of all companies in the area. Westport was considered a good example. Ivan thought that it would be better that the manager should first do some detailed market research on the golf market, activity market, walking market and cycling market in Ireland and the UK and possibly some focus on the US (with the help of Fáilte Ireland). This was in order to segment the markets as much as possible and identify distribution channels. Padraig recalled the great difficulty the company had over the years in increasing sales and awareness in the market due to the lack of capital in the company and that the company had always worked on marketing by cultivating relationships with opinion-formers and maintaining a high quality product. He mentioned the recent book written by John Garrity, the renowned *Sports Illustrated* golf writer on his quest to play the 17th hole in Carne, as an example of this type of marketing.

Joe said that marketing was an important element of the manager's job but that it was a very difficult area. He did his research and was interested in market growth strategies of market penetration, market development, product development and diversification. However, as he had been a member of the interview panel, he wished to confirm that the new manager had a high level of expertise in marketing and that this was a key skill set that the manager would bring to the company.

He highlighted the importance of having a unique selling proposition (USP) for the product, bringing value to the customer and having a defined marketing strategy before a web presence is developed. He said, for example, do walking societies have annual outings and, if they do, what information do they require in order to make a decision to walk in a certain area? Do they want to book online? What is special about the walks in Erris? What value could the company bring to the product offering? What and who was the competition? Could we provide a better quality product? Could we encourage the local trade to innovate new products for these markets? What kind of budget should be allocated to marketing? How could it be measured? Did we have a social media strategy? Should we develop customer relationship marketing (CRM) programmes, especially with key tour operators?

Joe acknowledged that the Board of the company lacked expertise in marketing and that he hoped that Micheal, Sean and Louise could help the company in this area. Micheal said that, whilst he was not an expert on marketing, that he had learned a lot over the years and hoped to help the company in any way he could. He suggested that the new marketing committee recommended by the strategic review be set up. Louise and Sean agreed to help on that committee, Padraig said that he also would join the committee and Micheal agreed to chair it. They all knew that this was probably the biggest single challenge the company and, indeed, the area had and that the first priority was to develop one overarching brand with strong values that would promote the area but, more importantly, that all the trade could identify with.

Micheal suggested that a local effort be made to put a marketing fighting fund together. This was a good idea but had to be thought out before being developed and maybe that the manager would have some ideas on this. Louise suggested that this would be explored with the manager when she was appointed.

Financial Control

Padraig was worried about how to control the cost of a marketing programme and that the company was going to lose money in the current year (currently projected at €30,000, with revenue projected to drop to €367,000). Sales had dropped from €452,000 in 2008 to €393,000 (including the extra €30,000 contribution from Belmullet Golf Club) in 2009. Sales to date in 2010 were lagging behind 2009. The major cost cutting programme undertaken in 2009 resulted in savings of €93,000, mostly by reducing staff hours and letting the Secretary Manager go in August 2009, as the company could no longer afford the cost. It was likely that the same level of staffing would have to be managed in 2010.

The projected profit for 2009 was €14,000, in comparison with a €42,000 operating loss in 2008. The work was mostly done by the finance committee and the successful extension of the interest-only arrangement with the bank on the €500,000 loan for the new development that was taken out in 2006 helped the cashflow position. However, it was likely that some capital would have to be paid in 2010 on the loan and this was likely to put pressure on the cashflow. He hoped that this wouldn't put the company in danger, but it had the potential to do so if the repayments the bank would want were too high. Therefore, the budget for marketing could not be increased in 2010 from the level in 2009 (€15,000)

The €150,000 (over a three-year period) from the local development fund was much needed to pay for the manager, but there was no fat in it when the wages of the manager was deducted. The funding was unlikely to be available in three years' time, so the new manager would have to increase sales by at least €200,000 *per annum* for the company to be able to sustain a manager. Joe raised the point that the company was employing a full-time manager. Some of the long-term staff were on short-time. This needed to be handled well or it could lead to some resentment. The meeting asked Joe to think how this could best be handled and make suggestions at the next executive meeting.

Padraig said that, in reality, the tourism development activities of the company had to be separated from the golf complex and to be fair to everybody, that there would have to be separate budgets, cashflows etc. He said that it was the responsibility of the finance committee to do this but that, if this was the road the company was going, the accounting systems had to be set up as two business units. It was agreed that the finance committee would develop two separate budgets.

Tom looked at his watch. It was after 8pm and he had to get home for dinner. Louise said she had another appointment with the hotel owner at 8.30pm. Joe said that he thought that a lot of positive discussion had taken place and that he had a good idea of the various roles that the manager would have to consider. Joe said that the changes suggested in the contract as a result of the meeting and, in particular, the roles of the manager, were complex but that he would incorporate what was agreed at the meeting into the contract. He reminded people that there could be some changes that the manager might want in the contract but that he would be prepared to complete the contract and agree it with the chairman of the company before having it signed. Tom said that this was a complex matter but that he had every faith that Joe would take the points of the meeting on board and suggested that he be allowed to complete the process (obviously with the chairman agreeing before final sign-off). Micheal said that he was glad a man of Joe's ability was prepared to do this and seconded Tom's proposal. Everybody else agreed and the meeting finished. Padraig suggested that everybody should come to the bar for a drink or a coffee for 15 minutes as a lot of work was done that evening. Everybody agreed.

The Importance of Government Policy

An important strategy document for tourism was published by the Irish Government in 2003 entitled *New Horizons for Irish Tourism: An Agenda for Action 2003 to 2012*. The group producing the report was chaired by Mr Maurice Pratt and included many experienced individuals in the tourism industry. It recognised tourism as a major industry for the Irish economy.

In November 2001, the Government, through the Department of Tourism, Culture and Sport, established the new National Development Authority which is now commonly known as Fáilte Ireland. Fáilte Ireland, working with Tourism Ireland, which is a North-South body, formed as a result of the Good Friday Agreement, co-operates in the development of tourism on the whole island of Ireland.

The current 2010 mission of Fáilte Ireland is: "To increase the contribution of tourism to the economy by facilitating the development of a competitive and profitable tourism industry". Some key priorities were listed in the 2010 Report and need to be considered by the new manager:

- Increase the top line and better manage the cost base.
- Development and delivery of a number of destination enterprise programmes.
- To apply for some of the €20 million set aside for capital support for tourism attractions and events.
- To facilitate innovation in tourism.
- To launch the biggest home holiday marketing programme in 2010.
- To facilitate tourism advisory, training and development.

CONCLUSION – THE SUN SHINES THROUGH THE CLOUDS

Half way through his coffee, Padraig got an email from 18 Swedish golfers on his Blackberry (since the previous manager left, he had diverted all out of hours emails to his Blackberry). They wanted to play Carne in April after seeing an offer on the website, but wished to visit Ireland for a week and asked could he make a few suggestions. He looked around, usually he would suggest a visit or activities in other parts of the West of Ireland. He asked Sean would the Gateway be open in April, asked Micheal if UISCE was open and checked accommodation with Louise. He started a quick reply to the query:

Dear Olaf, I'm currently unable to forward you a complete itinerary, but will email you tomorrow with a suggested itinerary based on your visit to Carne. We have many facilities, good accommodation and many activities available in April for your group. I have confirmed your golf booking on the days you requested. If you have any specific interest in water sports, walking, cycling, leisure activities, please let me know and we will forward a few suggestions. Thanking you for your enquiry. Padraig.

QUESTIONS

1. During the initial start up phase (1984-1993) of this 'Community Tourism Project', identify four significant factors unique to many 'Community Enterprise Projects'.

2. Outline the main strategic and operational challenges faced by the Board of 'Community Tourism Holdings' in phase 2 of the project.

3. The Board asked RBK Consultants to conduct a strategic review in late 2006. This report was delivered in 2008 but it was not until 2009 that the Board implemented the recommendations. Comment on the recommendations and the delay in the context of strategic management.

4. Based on the company's performance 2004-2008 (see **Table 10.1**), evaluate the strategy focus and analyse the key revenue and expenditure performance indicators.

5. Reviewing the two organisational charts (pre and post Strategic Review), it is noticeable that the strategic focus changed. Discuss.

6. A new manager has been appointed to the company, this is the third time that a manager is being appointed by the company. Outline the main challenges from a change management perspective that the manager is likely to face.

7. The Tourism Development Plan in June 2009 identified a number of specific market growth initiatives. Using marketing theory, how can the organisation grow and specifically what initiatives were proposed and implemented in the 2009 plan? Identify the role played by external bodies.

8. The company has developed a capacity for developing new products with the new tourism committee. Outline the processes that the company should engage in to foster innovation and new product development.

9. There are a number of major challenges, especially marketing, facing the new manager. Compile a shortlist of the challenges that she is likely to encounter upon her appointment.

11

WHERE THERE'S A WILL, THERE'S A WAY: THE STORY OF THE LIFESTART FOUNDATION

Doireann O'Connor

Educating parents, developing children

Lifestart

CASE SYNOPSIS

The Lifestart Foundation is a well-established, Irish-based but international, social innovation project that carries out quality educational work with children and young families. Its aim is to support child development to the extent that difficulties and issues that might have arisen without the impact of the service are prevented. Benefits such as early detection of physical or developmental delay, as well as social and behavioural education and support, resulting in less anti-social behaviour and more school preparedness, are common results of this early preventative intervention work.

One challenge it faces is the constant pressure to justify this approach. There is a limited amount of funding available for children and families and it often needs to justify why investment in preventing crises for all families is better than waiting for crisis to arise and then offering targeted support to those families in crisis.

The foundation is funded by a cocktail of social and public funders and maintaining current funding and accessing new funding is a constant challenge. Growth and development is also a constant priority for the foundation, especially as its research shows that its service is badly needed throughout Ireland and greatly benefits the families who are fortunate enough to be offered it. With growth comes change and the foundation is always operating in a change environment, which creates issues for the standardisation of the service and its support materials as it grows.

INTRODUCTION

At the end of another busy week in The Lifestart Foundation's head office in Northern Ireland, Pauline – the organisation's Executive Director – found herself working late preparing a conference paper on *Supporting Transitions in The Early Years*. The conference was scheduled to be held in Scotland and was focused on the broad topic of 'Family Support'. Governmental and non-governmental policy agencies, as well as numerous community organisations and prominent voluntary organisations, were scheduled to attend. Conferences, Pauline smiled to herself, were a great way of making new contacts. You never knew what kind of trickle-down effect those contacts had on an organisation's development. After all, it was at a conference that The Lifestart Foundation had been approached by Sister Mary Cudden of the Sisters of Mercy in Zambia. A friendly conversation and the discovery of a shared passion had resulted in the establishment of The Lifestart Foundation

Project in Mazabuka, Zambia, a highly successful project that now operated from 13 centres. Yes, indeed, thought Pauline, who knows who I'll meet at this conference.

Pausing to answer the phone, the expression on Pauline's face changed from one of satisfaction to one of thoughtful pensiveness as the conversation progressed. A UK government decision to transfer responsibility for children from their current policy home to a new department had been relayed to her by a friendly contact in her local government offices. This was a big issue, sighed Pauline to herself. For years now, The Lifestart Foundation had received stable state funding for their services to children in Northern Ireland. Transferring the responsibility for children to a whole new section of government would mean developing a whole new funding pitch for the potential new funders. New contacts and relationships would have to be made, built, nurtured. Pauline sighed heavily again as it struck her that the task would also involve *educating* the new funders about the preventative nature of The Lifestart Foundation's work. This couldn't have come at a more challenging time, thought Pauline. With both countries in the worst recession in living memory, being a publicly-funded body was getting increasingly difficult. There was just less money to go around and funders tended to place greater importance on crisis projects than preventative ones. Why couldn't they see the benefit of working to prevent them happening in the first place? "Ah well". thought Pauline, resolutely, "I've convinced others, I'll convince these too". Feeling the fortitude of determination re-energising her, Pauline finished her first draft of the conference paper and started to make her traditional *Friday Evening To Do List*, a practice that meant she started every Monday morning with focus and direction. This evening's list, she noted as she finished it, was really a wish list for the development of the organisation. Change, she said to herself, was definitely afoot. But then again ... wasn't it always.

PAULINE'S 'TO DO' LIST

1. Prepare a pitch for potential new funders with particular reference to the benefits of preventative services.

2. Think of new ways to make money, self-sustaining ways, ways that mean that we at The Lifestart Foundation can spend the money where we see fit rather than in funder-directed ways.

3. Establish a working group on standardisation; we need to fully standardise all we do across all services.

4. Develop an expansion plan for Northern Ireland.

5. Develop an expansion plan for the Republic of Ireland.

6. Write the following letters:

   - To the publishers of *The Growing Child* to thank them for expanding our publishing rights for 50 years in the EU, Macedonia, Zambia, Kenya and Japan.

   - To Professor Miyazaki and Professor Kendo Otaka of Seigakuin University in Japan in response to their recent request and confirm that they are welcome to base themselves in the foundation in the coming months as they research improving outcomes for children internationally.

   - To Sister Mary Cudden of the Sisters of Mercy in Mazabuka, Zambia, to get an update on the progress of our 13 projects there, and to arrange a timeframe to send a team over to update the African staff team's training.

7. Having decided that Scotland's policies on children's services are very in line with The Lifestart Foundation ethos, put some thought into how to make some policy connections in Scotland to start a mainland UK expansion plan there.

8. Establish a working group on international expansion. Where should we target first? What protocol for development will we follow?

ABOUT THE LIFESTART FOUNDATION

Lifestart is a home-based, educational and family support programme offered by The Lifestart Foundation. The programme works to support parents to enable their children to reach their full potential. Monthly, age-appropriate, child development material is delivered in the home by trained family visitors to parents throughout the first five years of the child's life.

The material used is based on a programme called 'The Growing Child'. This programme developed out of solid research on child development from a multi-disciplinary approach. All family visitors receive ongoing training to ensure that they remain up-to-date with new information and educational trends. They work with the parent(s) on all aspects of their child's development, including physical, intellectual, emotional and social development.

The Lifestart Programme is offered to all parents with a child aged from birth to 5 years regardless of socio-economic, educational or other backgrounds.

Many Lifestart Foundation projects also offer group activities for parents or parents and their children. For example, they offer courses such as *Creative Parenting*, which teaches parents how to support their child's artistic and musical development. Other courses that are regularly run include *Children's Self Esteem, Conflict Resolution, Behaviour Management, Nutrition*, and *Safety in the Home* etc.

At present, The Lifestart Foundation is active in the Republic of Ireland, Northern Ireland, Macedonia and Zambia.

The Background

The Lifestart Foundation is a National Voluntary Organisation, run by a committee of volunteers.

It started early in the 1980s when a school teacher – Sister Delores McGuinness – voiced her mounting concerns about the cyclical nature of disadvantage. Finding herself teaching the children of past pupils and countering the exact same issues led her to voice these concerns. Her audience was child development academics within the University of Ulster. This discussion led to the formation of a committee to examine the issue and seek a solution. After a research period, which included the discovery of 'The Growing Child' Programme, then an American programme delivered through a newsletter format to family homes, the group decided to adapt it to an Irish context and deliver it through a personable home visitation system aimed at supporting young families. Two small communities piloted this home visitation programmes. The first community was a rural Gaeltacht community in the west of Ireland and the second was an urban Northern Ireland community, deeply affected by the political conflict. The two projects worked collaboratively to bring a unified programme to their respective communities. Over time, collaboration merged into unity and the two projects became a single cross-border project called The Lifestart Foundation. From those initial conversations to the establishment of the Lifestart Foundation as we know it today had taken 20 years. This timeframe allowed for a high level of research and considered development, which, through its thoroughness, led to the establishment of the organisation based on very strong foundations. As its focus is also on the early childhood *foundation* years, it is exceptionally aptly named – The Lifestart Foundation.

Over the following 20 years, the foundation sought and received funding and volunteer support to become a nationwide body. There are currently 20 Lifestart projects internationally, including those based here in Ireland. The breakdown of the 20 projects is as follows: 11 single projects in the Republic of Ireland, seven single projects and one triple-based project in Northern Ireland, one project with 13 centres in Mazabuka, Zambia and one project with fifty centres in Macedonia.

The Lifestart Foundation is now a highly respected and viable social project, supporting the employment of nearly 20 staff members and a similar number of volunteers. The Lifestart services are collectively delivering support to the parents of 13,000 children.

The Product

The product is a parent learning programme, based on local adaptations of 'The Growing Child'. This published programme is a parent-directed but child-centred learning programme aimed at parents of children aged birth to five years old. The information contained within the programme is not normally available to parents but is available to health and other professionals working with children or providing children's services. The original 'Growing Child' product was developed by academics and child development experts. It has been subjected to regular review and updated in accordance with international trends in best practice. It is currently in its 5th edition. The Growing Child Program is offered in America through a newsletter system. Hence, the way it is offered in Ireland – through The Lifestart Foundation's Home Visitation Service – is unique.

The Service

The Lifestart Foundation promotes, develops and adapts 'The Growing Child' to the changing needs of contemporary Irish families. It is then delivered through a home visitor who visits the family home once a month and provides the parents with age-specific information on their child's development. The service starts at birth and continues until the child's fifth birthday. This longitudinal commitment to the family ensures continuity of quality informational support throughout the foundation years of every Lifestart child. The foundation works with local community groups to employ the family visitors. It supports the groups in harnessing locally-appropriate funding, provides guidance during recruitment and selection phases, provides staff training and ongoing development to both family visitors and the community groups hosting them, provides the locally-adapted 'Growing Child' programme and responds to needs identified by the groups on an ongoing basis. The foundation is also committed to ongoing evaluation and development of its service. No other organisation offers a service such as that of The Lifestart Foundation.

The Organisational and Staffing Structure

The Lifestart Foundation is managed by a voluntary Board of Directors, known as The Lifestart Foundation Council. The Board members are chosen for their skill-sets, as in any voluntary organisation. Members include children's services practitioners, policy-makers and skilled professions, such as an accountant, among others.

The Board of Directors seek advice on the ongoing evaluation study to impact development from an expert advisory panel made up of international policy-makers, academics and child development experts. These panel members come from all over the UK, the Republic of Ireland, the Netherlands and the US. The daily management of the foundation is run by Pauline McClenaghan, the executive director. Pauline is supported in her role by a team of managers, including a National Manager, an administrative and evaluation manager and a training and accreditation manager.

The management team are supported in their work by a team of support workers including regional development officers, parent education facilitators, training and accreditation officers, training and promotional officers and finance officers.

The management and support Teams are supported by an administrative team that includes administrators, receptionists and clerical workers.

Within the projects where the family visitors are based on a localised level, there is

- A local voluntary committee, hosting the local Lifestart project.
- A project manager.
- A co-ordinator.
- A family visitor team leader.
- A team of family visitors.

Lifestart's organisation structure is shown in **Figure 11.1**.

Figure 11.1: Lifestart Foundation's Organisational Chart

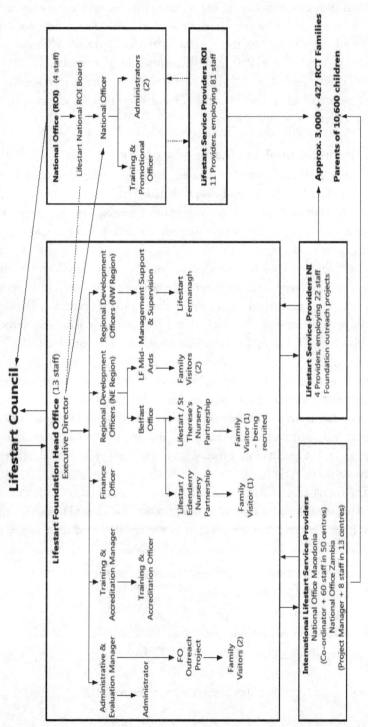

EXISTING CONNECTIONS AND PARTNERSHIPS

Many partnerships and connections are necessary to make a social venture work and The Lifestart Foundation have put a lot of effort into creating a wide range of international connections that provide support through networking and information links. **Figure 11.2** outlines these connections.

Figure 11.2: Lifestart Foundation and Its Existing Partnerships

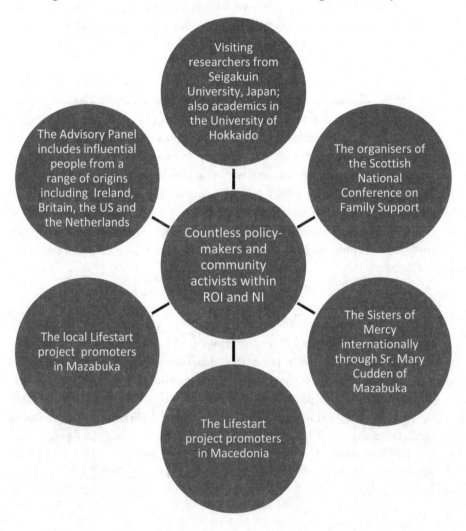

The Brand

The colour blue was chosen as the colour of The Lifestart Foundation, due to its connotations with gentleness, care and kindness. A restful and universally-liked colour, it topped the poll in a survey of The Lifestart Foundation staff. The colour is used in the logo, on letterheads, business cards, compliment slips, embroidered polo shirts given to all staff and all materials representing The Lifestart Foundation.

The image in the logo of a tree represents the Tree of Life. It aims to reflect natures nurturing for growth and development. It is The Lifestart Foundation's belief that nurturing is what helps children to reach their full potential.

Upon the Tree, different fruits and acorns are present. Their difference represents children's differences in terms of talents, skills, interests, development outcomes and so on. It embodies the philosophy of individuality within care and education. The acorn represents a reminder that each child may also grow into a tree to bear fruit of its own. This cycle of life is very important within the Lifestart philosophy, as children will nurture as they have been nurtured. Positive childhood experiences in this generation have far-reaching effects for the next generation.

Finally, Lifestart is based at the roots of the Tree where it supports parents to create a home learning environment that maximises child development potential.

The Philosophy

The Lifestart Foundation philosophy is one of prevention rather than cure. It seeks to support families before problems occur as a result of lack of support. In this way, it seeks to stop potential difficulties developing in the first place. This can be a difficult philosophy to garner funding for. It's not that anyone disagrees with it as a philosophy, it's just that crisis situations or 'cure' type services are so critical in their urgency that it is a challenge to divert funders focus on what could be done to prevent the crises in the first place. The Lifestart Foundation has adopted a parable that underpins its philosophy and explains it very well. It is outlined in **Appendix 1**, *The Parable of Early Intervention*.

KEY ISSUES TO BE CONSIDERED

Continue to Ensure and Increase the Quality of the Service

Quality is defined by the foundation as meeting the needs of its service users. In order to reach this goal, it must regularly research the changing needs of its service users and potential service users in order to ensure that the quality of service is meeting current needs. This necessitates an ongoing research aspect to the foundation's work.

At present, a well-funded research strand to its work is being undertaken as a result of funding from Atlantic Philanthropies. As such, this priority is well-served for the short to medium term. Once completed, however, it is merely a matter of time before a further research need will arise. The foundation needs to remain focused on research as a continuing and perpetuating need and to plan long-term for its sustainability as a constant component of quality assurance.

The Standardisation of Materials

Due to the organisational structure of The Lifestart Foundation and the involvement at local level of diverse community groups and numerous local partnerships, there has inevitably been a dilution of standardisation over the years. Examples include photocopying of materials without logos, diverse quality of training being offered to family visitors in various locations, variations in the resources and toys that family visitors bring on family visits and other such issues relating to standardisation that The Lifestart Foundation has recently identified and is currently focused on addressing.

Funding

The foundation operates using a cocktail of funding avenues. Its primary source of revenue comes from the Health Service Executive, which habitually supports its services throughout the Republic of Ireland using Community Care, Family Support and Drug Task Force funding to do so. This funding comes with a grave recognition of the preventative nature of the work of the foundation. In Northern Ireland, it receives consistent financial support through both the Health Trusts and 'Surestart' – a government project aimed at early childhood support, the Health Trusts having been traditionally the major funding source. This funding is currently in focus as the responsibility for children has recently been transferred from the Health Trusts to the Department of Education and new relationships must therefore be established.

In addition to these funding sources, it receives finance from Co. Offaly and Co. Kildare Vocational Education Committees (VECs), some Dublin-based FÁS services and some Dublin-based RAPID (Revitalising Areas by Planning, Investment and Development) programmes.

The Lifestart Foundation's commitment to ongoing evaluation and development is met through a Cross National Research and Development Strategy which is funded by Atlantic Philanthropies – a philanthropic organisation that funds projects aiming to combat disadvantage. This allows the Lifestart Foundation to carry out research, which is an important source of information and serves to guide the quality of the product and service that it offers.

Current funding priorities are:

- To maintain current levels of funding in the Republic of Ireland despite the economic downturn and the resulting strain on public resources.
- To stabilise current funding in Northern Ireland as new government structures have changed the remit of its traditional funding body.
- To seek alternative, more independent, funding to allow for self-sustainability.

In the Republic of Ireland, Lifestart services have been affected by budget cuts imposed by the Health Service Executive (HSE), which purchases the service through annually-renewed service level agreements with Lifestart projects. The latest budget (Budget 2010) gave rise to considerable reductions in the funds available to the HSE, which in turn is likely to involve further cuts to service provider budgets. These reductions are occurring at a time when preventive interventions such as the Lifestart programme are most needed, in that parenting education and family support have been shown to reduce the impact of poverty and parental stress on child development outcomes, thereby reducing the impact of the economic downturn on children. The Foundation is attempting to deal with this funding crisis by endeavouring to restructure service provision on a regional basis with the view to reducing delivery, management and administration costs.

Future Growth and Development

The Lifestart Foundation and its service providers in Ireland have recently completed an envisioning exercise aimed at identifying barriers to the growth of the Lifestart service in Ireland and at addressing issues of long-term sustainability and development. In 2005, it drew up a strategic plan for the future growth and development of The Lifestart Foundation. It applied for, and was granted, finance from Atlantic Philanthropies to begin a longitudinal evaluation of the Lifestart programme, the idea being that all future growth will be based on solid information relating to the impact of the Lifestart service on participants.

A pilot evaluative study was carried out in 2005/2006 and a revised development strategy and methodology for the full scientific testing of Lifestart outcomes were agreed in June 2007. As part of its strategic development, the Foundation is working to expand service delivery through the development of a range of programme delivery modes and partnerships. Recruitment of 500 families to participate in a random control trial of programme impact began in April 2008. Interim study findings will be published in September 2010, and again in January 2013, with full study findings being published in 2014. The research is being carried out in collaboration with the Institute of Childcare Research at Queens University and the Centre for Effective Education, also at Queens University, Belfast.

The Foundation's expansion plans are based on the preliminary findings of the research, which sees a need for both the expansion of the foundation's work within its existing national bases and also its development in other countries. The initial expansion plans include all communities within the Republic of Ireland and Northern Ireland, as well as establishment in mainland Britain, additional areas of Africa and Japan. Longer term expansion plans also include mainland Europe.

Current development priorities are:

- To expand the number of services within the Republic of Ireland.
- To expand the number of services within Northern Ireland.
- To expand the number of services internationally, using as a starting point the existing international connections in countries where copyright and publishing agreement has been reached.

PAULINE'S 'TO DO' LIST - REVISITED

1. **Prepare a pitch for potential new funders, with particular reference to the benefits of preventative services:** This will involve research into the benefits of preventative services as an alternative to waiting until a crisis situation occurs and only then seeking to address it retrospectively. Having completed literature-based research into this topic, a short and attention-

grabbing presentation will need to be prepared based on no more than 10 main points that really underpin the value of preventative services. The focus of the presentation should be an equal blend of ethical and financial underpinnings. The ethical underpinnings should focus on how humanitarian preventative aid is, as it prevents families and children experiencing crises that are, by their nature, damaging and traumatic. The financial underpinnings should show the cost/benefit analysis of preventative services *versus* crisis management services. An excellent reference source for such underpinnings is the American research project, The Perry Preschool Project, which details hard financial data on how cost-effective preventative services are in relation to young children.

2. **Think of new ways to make money, self-sustaining ways, ways that mean that we at The Lifestart Foundation can spend the money where we see fit rather than in funder-directed ways:** Raising sustainable finance is a constant issue for The Lifestart Foundation. Students and student groups who identify ideas for fundraising are invited to contact Pauline directly via The Lifestart Foundation website. Some possibilities include publishing short booklets on topics for parents such as age-related play activities. A potential target market for these could be the County Childcare Committees and Family Resource Centres that exist in every county. It is conceivable that they may consider buying these in bulk to distribute to the parents they support. A wide range could be developed based on the unique knowledge contained within The Lifestart Foundation. A similar range of more academic publications could be developed aimed at students and marketed through the VECs and FÁS, which run Further Education and Training Award Council-accredited courses in early childhood care and education, as well as the Institutes of Technology and universities, which run Higher Education and Training Award Council-accredited courses and degrees in early childhood care and education. A further possibility worth exploring is the development of a similar service to the one currently run, but aimed at affluent parents instead of disadvantaged ones and offered on a pay-for-service basis. On a system where the not-for-profit ethos was maintained, it is conceivable that such a pay-for service type could subsidise the service for families that could not afford it.

3. **Establish a working group on standardisation; we need to fully standardise all we do across all services:** This is essentially a logistical operation. An audit of existing resources may be required as a starting point, including an audit of materials and an audit of family visitor

training. Policies on branding and using standardised materials are also required here.

4. **Develop an expansion plan for Northern Ireland and for the Republic of Ireland:** These tasks essentially involve reaching community groups on the ground that would be willing to become partners with The Lifestart Foundation in the roll-out of its service. A pitch for these community groups should include a presentation, where existing community partners talk about how beneficial the partnership approach has been for them. Case studies of families who benefited from the service would also work well as part of this pitch. A DVD might be a good way to showcase these multi-layered benefits. A marketing strategy of identifying appropriate community groups and ensuring that they engage with the promotional material is needed. Nearly every county council has a full contact directory for all community and voluntary groups active in the county available through their community and enterprise section or their county development office. Every county also has a community forum where members from key community groups are represented. The community forums meet regularly and generally welcome presentations.

4. **Write the following letters:**
   o To the publishers of *The Growing Child* to thank them for expanding our publishing rights for 50 years in the EU, Macedonia, Zambia, Kenya and Japan.
   o To Professor Miyazaki and Professor Kendo Otaka of Seigakuin University in Japan in response to their recent request and confirm that they are welcome to base themselves in the foundation in the coming months as they research improving outcomes for children internationally.
   o To Sister Mary Cudden of The Sisters of Mercy in Mazabuka, Zambia, to get an update on the progress of our 13 projects there, and to arrange a timeframe to send a team over to update the African staff team's training.

This section of the list essentially highlights key areas where international expansion could be explored. Zambia and Japan are both highlighted as countries with existing contacts and full publishing rights for The Lifestart Foundation materials. Sister Mary Cudden in Zambia could be contacted with a view to exploring the expansion of The Lifestart Foundation projects to other areas in Zambia. It is conceivable that she will have contacts, perhaps through the Sisters of Mercy, in other regions of Zambia.

Japan is also a strong contender here for international expansion. The academic contacts are about to become even stronger as the professors are to be based at The Lifestart Foundation offices for a research period. It is a clear opportunity to explore expansion into Japan via these contacts. They could possibly arrange for a meeting with Japanese public service funders. The funding pitch developed as task number 1 of this list could be adapted easily for a Japanese funding audience.

5. **Having decided that Scotland's policies on children's services are very in line with The Lifestart Foundation ethos, put some thought into how to make some policy connections in Scotland to start a mainland UK expansion plan there:** This also involves gaining access to public service funders and making a successful pitch. In the introduction, we saw Pauline preparing a conference paper for a conference in Scotland on the topic of Family Support. This conference offers an opportunity to Pauline to make a key connection with someone who will help to pave her pathway into making a pitch to Scottish-based public funding policy agencies. This needs to be a priority agenda for the duration of the conference. Presenting a paper will inevitably present her with networking opportunities to achieve this goal.

6. **Establish a working group on international expansion. Where should we target first? What protocol for development will we follow?** Pauline needs support within her organisation to achieve the goal of international expansion. A working group is a good idea in this context. Its recruitment could include interested members of both staff and management committees. However, a working group needs terms of reference in order to stay focused on what they are trying to achieve. Terms of reference includes identifying where they will target for international expansion. What timeframe they envisage it happening in for each instance should also be included, as well as a breakdown of the tasks involved for each expansion plan into specific countries.

QUESTIONS

1. From what you read about Sister Delores and Pauline, what do you think are the personality traits of the successful social entrepreneur?

2. Do you think the ideas for making revenue that are outlined in Pauline's 'to do' list revisited section are ethical for a social entrepreneurship project?

3. What kind of issues might arise in an organisation with this level of ongoing change?

4. What steps could this organisation take to bring a more standardised approach to its operations?

5. Can you think of any ideas to harness ongoing funding for sustainable research that will allow The Lifestart Foundation to continue ongoing research as a quality enhancement measure on a long-term basis?

6. How should Pauline achieve her networking goal at the upcoming Scottish conference?

APPENDIX 1: THE LIFESTART FOUNDATION PHILOSOPHY: *A PARABLE OF EARLY INTERVENTION*

Once upon a time, there was a small village at the edge of a river.

The people there were good people and life in the village was good.

One day, a villager noticed a baby floating down the river; she jumped in and swam out to save the baby from drowning.

The next day, she noticed two babies in the river. She called for help and both babies were rescued.

The following day there were four babies caught in the turbulent current, then eight, then more and still more.

The villagers quickly organised themselves, setting up watchtowers and training teams of swimmers who could resist the swift waters and rescue the babies.

Rescue squads were soon working 24 hours a day and each day the number of helpless babies floating down the river increased.

While all the babies, now very numerous, could not be saved, the villagers felt that they were doing very well to save as many as possible and they continued on that basis.

One day, however, someone raised the question: "But where are all these babies coming from? Who is throwing them into the river? Why? Let's organise a team to go upstream and see who's doing it".

The seeming logic of the elders countered: "And if we go upstream who will operate the rescue operations? We need every concerned person here?".

"But don't you see" cried the lone voice, "if we find who is throwing them in, we can stop the problem and no babies will drown. By going upstream to the source, we can eliminate the problem."

"It is too risky".

And so the number of babies in the river increased daily. Those saved increased but those who drown increase even more.

Source: McCormack. T. (1989) Approaches to Family and Community Education. Proceedings of the conference – Education for Family and Community Development. CMRS Education Office

This parable underpins The Lifestart Foundation Philosophy. Its core mission is in *prevention*. They place themselves firmly metaphorically upriver and seek to reduce the number of babies ending up in the river.